Shaking Wolves
Out Of
Cherry Trees

And 149
Other Sermon Ideas

Terry Cain

CSS Publishing Company, Inc., Lima, Ohio

SHAKING WOLVES OUT OF CHERRY TREES

Copyright © 2002 by
CSS Publishing Company, Inc.
Lima, Ohio

Library of Congress Cataloging-in-Publication Data

Cain, Terry, 1938-
    Shaking wolves out of cherry trees : and 149 other sermon ideas / Terry Cain.
        p. cm.
Includes index.
    ISBN 0-7880-1947-3 (pbk. : alk. paper)
    1. Sermons—Outlines, syllabi, etc. I. Title.
BV4223 .A29 2003
251'.02—dc21
                                                                    2002013737

For more information about CSS Publishing Company resources, visit our website at www.csspub.com or e-mail us at custserv@csspub.com or call (800) 241-4056.

ISBN 0-7880-1947-3   PRINTED IN U.S.A.

This book is dedicated to my family:

My late father, Harold Cain
My late mother, Dorothy Cain
My wife, Sue Cain
My son, Terry Cain
My daughter, Sherry Clements
My son-in-law, Dan Clements

Acknowledgments

My profuse thanks to Jerry McInnis, a retired United Methodist minister and colleague, who with his proofreading expertise helped to render this manuscript readable. Because he has a strong theological background and is an outstanding preacher himself, he was also able to point out ideas that needed clarification. Any mistakes or unclear thoughts remain because I failed to correct the text successfully after he spotted the confusion.

The congregations who suffered through the preaching of these ideas over the years deserve your sympathy and my sincere thanks. They were always so kind and supportive. I will put a positive spin on the tears they shed at my leaving and try not to suspect they were tears of relief accompanied by a silent prayer of, "Thank God this era of our history is over!"

My wife Sue is always offering helpful suggestions and tolerant of the time my writing takes away from family time.

Table Of Contents

Introduction

I got *As* in preaching in seminary. You're not impressed? Neither were the congregations I preached to over the years. But I was impressed with my sermons despite my wife's criticisms directed towards keeping me humble.

One instance comes to mind. One Sunday morning early in my ministry I stumbled over a phrase. I stopped, repeated it, but it didn't come out right the second time either. I tried again with even less success. After a couple of additional attempts, I got it right and continued with the message. The congregation laughed after my first garbled attempt and each succeeding try, and continued to laugh even after I finally got it right. I was getting angry because their laughter was probably distracting their attention from the vital message I was sharing with them. On the way home I mentioned to my wife that the congregation was rude to continue laughing over my blunders as long as they did. She informed me that the last attempt was a failure too. What amused the congregation was that they could tell by the very pleased look on my face that I thought I finally got it right.

Purpose Of Book

This is a book of "sermon starters" (brilliant ones I might add): 150 titles with some preparation aids or suggestions. Each individual message has some ideas upon an important subject that each minister should be preaching about. The ideas and suggestions are just that — only suggestions. Each pastor may only find some seed (a phrase, idea, or illustration) from each sermon synopsis for growing her or his own message and ignore everything else regarding that title or subject, however much the latter would disappoint me.

Space prohibits more than just bare bones suggestions because of the attempt to include more than just a few sermons. This means that each subject needs a great deal of fleshing out which will send each preacher using one of these ideas off in her or his own direction. Once in a while I have included an abbreviated humorous story or an illustration. They may need added details supplied by you to make a proper story. I hope there is enough there for clarity.

Now that I am retired, it seems a terrible waste to let all this exciting and fantastic material disappear. Trust me, every preacher considers it a tragedy when any church member misses one of her or his great sermons. An absent parishioner will miss a message absolutely necessary for her or his well-being. It may be some time before the preacher returns to that subject, and (heavens!) that same parishioner might be absent that Sunday also.

The book is also intended to be used by any person, clergy or laity, as "starter" ideas for devotions at meetings (youth, women's, or men's groups) and, perhaps, as a book of personal devotions even for yourself. You know, those things you used to have time to do. (Of course, I see this book in aggregate as a profound theological statement.)

Sermon Titles

Each message idea contains a "catchy" title, suggested appropriate scripture, some possible points, or just simply two or three brief paragraphs to open up an idea. Under each title is always a purpose statement in *italics*. In this book the purpose statement is only intended to give the subject focus; whereas the purpose statement each pastor should use to organize the sermon would be an attempt to state just exactly what the sermon intends to accomplish. Occasionally, there will be a reference to some book that will be helpful.

When I say "catchy" titles, I hope you find them intriguing. I am a firm believer in using sermon titles that catch the attention. For example: a sermon on Matthew 7:15 concerning being sent out among wolves looking like sheep, one could use a title such as "Beware Of Growling Sheep." I hope each listener will wake up and say, "What in the world is this all about?" Enough cannot be said for anticipation and expectation. The intention is to get each person in the congregation started on the message before you get started. And even if you never do get "started," they have benefited over a little pre-preaching cogitation.

If there seem to be an inordinate number of titles in the form of questions, it is because I think a question helps elicit a response from the bulletin reader. Titles such as "What Made Jesus Cry?" and "What's The Matter With Sex?" should command some early attention. I dislike boring titles. "Build A Strong Faith" or "The Power Of Prayer" may be accurately descriptive of the message, but they do not promise anything new and worrisome. I occasionally visit a church on Sunday morning where there is no title for the sermon, just the word, "Sermon" or "Message," printed in the bulletin. An opportunity was missed, perhaps because procrastination caught the preacher until after the bulletin deadline.

Images that a title conjures up for the worshiper may be significant. It could be that concrete visions of familiar, interesting, and likeable objects are more pleasant to reflect upon instead of the more abstract ideas usually visited in most sermon titles. *Prayer, faith, hope,* and so forth are elusive to our mental grasps at best. Objects such as *whales, butterflies, cherry trees,* and *kisses* can be warm and friendly and welcome our reflection. *Frankenstein, garbage cans, graves,* and *dinosaurs* give us vivid grist for our imaginations. Pique our thoughts and you start with our attention and expectations.

Have there been any studies of this theme or is it too inconsequential to warrant considerations? Perhaps I'm dealing with the trivial here and we could all just numerically serialize our titles in the Sunday bulletin: Sermon #391, etc.

I truly hope that I have not inadvertently plagiarized anyone else's title. To my knowledge, all of these titles are original. However, coincidence is always possible. There is always a slight possibility that I saw an interesting title on a church marquee somewhere or a phrase in a book and unconsciously called it up to use at a later time. My apologies to you if I usurped one of your titles. Take consolation in the fact that though I used your title unconsciously, my use of it became an incomparable gem.

Ideas That Matter
I always wanted to preach on new, unique, and important subjects, or about common, familiar subjects in more exciting and creative ways. I probably never did, but my wife always said,

"You're doing just fine!" I dreaded preaching what every member of the congregation already knew and probably could do a better job of presenting than I could. Consequently, you know how hard it was for me to preach on occasions such as Thanksgiving or Mother's Day. What do you say concerning those subjects that hasn't already been said?

Some topics are extremely vital (prayer, salvation, forgiveness, etc.) but need an infusion of something attention-getting if the congregation is going to stay awake and with you for the entire hour or hour and a half, or however long your sermons are. Then there are the subjects about which they may hear very little and very seldom, for example, a message suggesting "God's Ways Won't Always Work" that details how the right way may sometimes fail. Or we can deal with the intriguing question, "Do You Have To Be Smart To Be A Christian?"

There are questions most people are asking and preachers may not be answering. Questions such as, "Why would a loving God allow such pain and suffering in a good world?" And, my friend, the answer to that one is not just the final solution found in Job. The book of Job simply tells us we can't know the inscrutable ways of God — so we must accept God's ways. I believe we can provide better answers by preaching a sermon like C-1, "What On Earth Is God Doing?" or H-1, "Good God Or Perfect Book" or I-10, "Why Do Lions Eat Lambs?" from this book. After you have given some possible explanations, *then* you can say, "There are some things about God's world and ways that we don't understand."

There are controversial subjects (abortion, capital punishment, etc.) that are totally ignored and shouldn't be. There may be a need occasionally to preach clarifying sermons to explain the theological subtleties of our hymns or affirmations. Are any of our members troubled by singing, "God will take care of you"? Do they need to know this doesn't mean if you accept Christ you won't have bad things happen to you, like getting cancer?

After one of our sermons a church member doesn't have to run out of church all on fire shouting, "I can move mountains!" But occasionally listeners should walk out of church saying, "I hadn't thought of that before."

Controversial Preaching

May I add some comments concerning preaching on "social issues" which usually translates into "controversial subjects"? I have included a few in the repertoire. It seems natural, though not necessarily safe, to stand by your denominational position statement on the subjects that might cause disagreement among the flock. Subjects such as capital punishment, prayer in the schools, gun control, or abortion will be inflammatory. It is probably wise to earn some tenure time before launching out on dangerous ground. By first establishing rapport with the membership, they will tolerate, if not agree, with your position. Let them get to know you and love you first. You are loveable, aren't you?

It is important to reach the members, not drive them away. You will never change their thinking when they are gone. However, if you are preaching the "full gospel," you may lose some members. Remember the rich young man who walked away disappointed with what Jesus asked of him and his possessions? The Old Testament prophets often made the people (religious people) angry enough to threaten or harm the prophets. Paul and other followers of Jesus had the same experience. Jesus himself lost his life because he dared to challenge the "religious folk" of his day. I suspect that people are not so very different today. If you don't disturb somebody sometime, you might just be trying to make everyone "feel good" and like you. Are you preaching the full gospel? Obviously, your intent is not to act the martyr or rile people up for the fun of it. You could save the controversial challenges for classes, bypassing the pulpit, but then you would miss a great many listeners.

You might be surprised at the potential effectiveness of preaching. I conducted an experiment on three occasions in a church of about 600 members. I preached on an issue on which I knew the congregation would generally hold a position opposite of my own. I had them vote on a ballot before the sermon and then again after the sermon. The subjects for those three Sundays were capital punishment, prayer and Bible reading in the schools, and racism. The results were very similar in all three cases. Here is one example:

15

first vote		second vote
47.4%	I favor the use of capital punishment for persons committing certain crimes.	29.7%
21.8%	I am undecided.	16.2%
30.8 %	I am opposed to the use of capital punishment under any circumstances.	54.0%

To my knowledge, in all my years of ministry, I only lost three families due to preaching on a controversial subject: One woman left because I spoke on abortion, and two couples (military families) in another church in the '60s left when I preached against our involvement in Vietnam. The two families told me they loved me, but could not attend that church again. If I were less of a coward, I might have lost many more. I believe that it illustrates that you can establish healthy, loving relationships with your church members who will listen to you, but not always agree.

"Biblical" Preaching

One criticism often floating around is that Sunday school material or the sermon is not biblical enough. While it is true one can stray entirely from any connection with scripture, perhaps it is more often the case that there might be two understandings of what constitutes biblical-related study or preaching. Some need a very simple Bible connection in order to recognize the relationship. The references to scripture must be in easily identifiable steps that children can manage. This isn't bad. Our message must always be clear and uncluttered. However, some people will be able to carry on a more sophisticated approach where biblical ideas are being examined without our resorting to a simple format such as: (a) This is Amos, (b) See Amos read the Bible, (c) God talks to Amos, (d) Now Amos is preaching to us.

Our preaching is not always restricted to a dissection of a verse or two. Sometimes we are talking about the nature of the church or what it means to be a Christian by more indirect references to scripture, ideas recognized as Christian or biblical. There is something to be said for the fact that we are adults and do not need to be talked down to. At the same time, it does seem that we are not always ready for "meat" and need to be "fed with milk" (Paul's terminology, 1 Corinthians 3:2).

Most of the messages in this book are more topical in nature than "biblical." Scripture is included in almost every case. However, these short one or two page "starters" are only germs or seeds that you may develop and make your own. You may choose scripture which you feel is more appropriate than that which I have included. If you choose to use one of these message titles and don't make it biblical enough to satisfy the customers, please don't mention my name.

I have a feeling that we preachers often start with scripture and dissect and analyze it for a message relevant for today as opposed to selecting an issue and then searching for scripture to match. We can fall into the trap of either "forcing points artificially to fit" a story or idea from scripture in order to be "biblical," or forcing scripture (or seeking desperately to find a scripture that relates in some distant way to the problem) to support our theme. In either case this may cause either a distortion of the interpretation of the scripture passage or a distortion in the flow of the message. For many listeners the only way a sermon will be biblical is for the preacher to start with a Bible passage and then find a message in it.

There is a parallel of this phenomenon when we follow the Lectionary. For the purpose of keeping pastors out of ruts and encouraging us to broaden our preaching to cover a wider range of subjects and scriptures (a very good concept), the Lectionary may force us to deal with something that isn't in our heart while we may be excited over another topic at the moment. This may cause us to feel guilty when we forego the Lectionary in order to deal with a current and relevant event such as a race incident in the community that needs addressing from the pulpit! I confess I never followed the Lectionary.

You will soon discover I have a predilection for the book of Matthew. I don't apologize for that. It is my conviction that, as Christian pastors, we must focus and concentrate on the teachings of Jesus! Jesus must remain central to our preaching and Matthew, for me, has the best presentation of Jesus and his teachings. If we

were forced to choose only one book from our Bible, I would select Matthew. And if you could magically transport The Good Samaritan (Luke 10), The Prodigal Son (Luke 15), and John 8:1-11
over into Matthew, I would promise always to be good.

Odds And Ends

Occasionally, when I preach I have been guilty of using my
unorthodox theory of sermon organization that I call the "popcorn"
style. I make a statement and illustrate it with a barrage of facts
and stories with no particular structure (such as the trinitarian sermon formula of three points). I never expect the listener to repro-
duce logically a sequence in, or flow to, the message later at home.
I only hope that she or he will remember the central theme or idea,
be impressed, and say, "Wow, the preacher really hit it from all
angles!" I haven't had any negative feedback on this method from
those in the congregations who remained awake. And anyway, I'm
out of reach of my homiletics professor's grading pencil.

There is an index of topics or subjects in the back of this book.
A particular message may be found under two or more listings.

There are ideas that may be better developed as series of sermons. They could include: "Why Do We Need God?" "Why Did
They Want Him To Die?" (which would look at the Jews, Roman
officials, soldiers, crowd, Judas, etc., and their reasons for wanting
Jesus to die) and "Does God Have Any Muslim (Hindu, Buddhist,
etc.) Friends?" (to examine other religions in comparison with
Christianity). Of course, some of the other messages throughout
this book could be expanded to become a series.

Conscientious preaching requires a certain amount of repetition. Certain subjects and ideas are far too important not to be repeated from time to time. One doesn't preach "the" definitive sermon on what salvation means or the power of prayer, and now it's
over. Even though there is a variety of things to be said on most
topics, we all need to keep coming back to those ideas that need
reiterating. I have tried to avoid repetition of points or ideas in
these messages; however, there is some inevitable overlapping in a
few instances.

18

These titles are free to use. The intention of the copyright is to prohibit any unauthorized reprint or sale of material. I hope you can find at least one title to use to make the $50 you paid for this book worthwhile. If you paid anything less than that, it was a steal. If you use any of these titles' ideas, you don't have to give me any credit. In fact, please don't mention my name — I don't need anyone else unhappy with me.

Preaching seems to me to be an ostentatious business, even if God did call us.

- Humility is a must.
- You'd better mean what you say.
- You don't have to give the impression that as a preacher you are perfect.
- It helps if the pain and agony of others make you cry once in a while.
- Humor helps.
- Preaching brings great joy and satisfaction at times.
- If you are not disappointed occasionally, you probably don't know what is going on.

A.

A-1. Shaking Wolves Out Of Cherry Trees

Purpose Statement: *Out of the many conflicting messages, how can we determine who is telling us the truth and who are the false prophets?*

Matthew 7:15-22. The comments of Jesus regarding wolves in sheep disguises raise a legitimate concern that is very relevant today. There are varieties of religions, and within the Christian religion itself, many denominations. The messages are sometimes at odds. Add to that possibility the fact that some of the religious leaders may be phonies, e.g. Elmer Gantrys. It is not easy to do a sermon on differentiating the truth from the fiction and fantasy that comes from our pulpits today. Some preachers, not knowing the truth, are "wolves" out of simple ignorance; others, very few we hope, are "wolves" through their duplicity.

Our church members are exposed to television and radio evangelists (many who are after their money) and need to differentiate the honest and true from the false. In the mixed metaphor, Jesus tells us we can know them by the fruit they bear. Sounds easy. What is that fruit and how do we know it is sound or good fruit? Some possibilities:

    a.   Success? Big crowds and growing churches are no indication. Compare the bars on a Saturday night near a college campus with the community blood bank the next day. Popularity and the size of the crowd do not necessarily reflect values. Jesus, Paul, and the prophets were disliked, threatened, and killed.

    b.   "Bible preaching" and God talk? Jesus said, "Not everyone who calls me, Lord, Lord...."

    c.   Personality? We often mistake this for "having the spirit."

    d.   Good deeds?

e. The only good test: Christians must build a "healthy" faith by immersing themselves in the nature of Jesus by assiduous study and prayer. Then measure everything with what is consistent with Jesus. The message should be one of sacrificial love, openness, healthy relationships, and not divisiveness.

A-2. Will God Help The St. Louis Cardinals Win?

Purpose Statement: *What are the appropriate and inappropriate subjects for prayer?*

Because we hear prayers for almost everything, and knowing that there are boundaries to the things we should pray for, this message would delineate the limits to proper and improper prayer requests. Praying for a victory for your favorite athletic team is out-of-bounds. Praying for courage to face a moral choice is a good prayer.

The ultimate answer to the question of what are we allowed to pray for is that "it must be in harmony with the will of God." And what is that will? The following might be main points of this message:

a. It must be a moral request. (i.e.: You cannot pray for harm for another person.)
b. It cannot contradict God's natural law. (i.e.: You do not seek to suspend gravity.)
c. It cannot be a selfish request.
d. It should be something you are willing to work for and become a part of the answer.

Scripture references: Luke 11:5-13, Matthew 17:19-20; 21:21-22. (When dealing with this subject, it would be important to clarify scriptures that can be misunderstood such as these.)

(Humorous illustration: A little girl who wasn't invited to her best friend's birthday picnic was told by her mom that the mislaid invitation had arrived at the last moment. The little girl said that it was too late, she had already prayed for rain.)

A-3. Do You Have To Be Smart To Be A Christian?

Purpose Statement: *Since the Bible isn't always easy to understand and the world is very complex, do we have to be smart or a serious student to understand what it takes to be a Christian?*

Matthew 7:7-8 and 10:16-20 are suggested scriptures.

This is not an easy question to answer. Yet, it is a question that should trouble every thoughtful pastor.

a. The answer is *yes* because the world confronts us with very complex issues. The Christian is forced to make decisions on issues that present an array of facts and logical reasons on both sides — not to mention emotion. Issues such as the death penalty, gun control, and abortion have many arguments to sort through. It would seem that too many of the social issues we face require a certain level of intelligence to find the path of truth. To accept the official position of your denominational connection would seem prudent, but we still want to think for ourselves.

b. The answer is *yes* because the Bible isn't easy to understand regarding many themes and only speaks indirectly on others. (Note message M-9 as just one example of the difficulty finding the appropriate biblical position on an issue.) Does the Bible preach pacifism or not? What about the use of alcohol? The church historically has literally fought and killed over arguments concerning the "nature" of Jesus.

Despite saying *yes* twice I would hasten to add:

c. The answer is *no* because I can't believe that God made it necessary to be intelligent (or be dependent on someone who is) to be a Christian. The answer is *no* also because there is another way. From the life and teachings of Jesus it is clear that love is greater than anything else. If we give ourselves over, more and more, to the power of love and prayerfully "ask, seek, and knock" it will be "given to us when the time comes." Love will lead us and cause us finally to "sense" that which is God's will. We can never

23

know perfectly in this life, but we can grow awfully close to God and an understanding of God's will. Intelligence (wise as serpents) is very good and important; however, love (peaceful as doves) is greater.

A-4. Daring To Be A Lion's Breakfast!

Purpose Statement: *Do we always have the necessary courage to take a moral stand or face ridicule, suffering, or sacrifice to be true to the Christian mandate?*

Use an appropriate scripture from Daniel to show how Daniel was willing to risk his life in order to be faithful to his God (perhaps Daniel 6:6-16). Begin with some background to Daniel's purported historical situation. One set of progressive thoughts might be:

    a.   Speak out. There are times when a word needs to be said, a letter written, or a protest demonstration conducted to call attention to some injustice or wrong. If anything, we are too reluctant to take the necessary stands to make a significant witness in our communities.

    b.   Speak out and be eaten. To raise a cry of injustice or make a moral statement means offending the parties benefiting from the injustice or wrong. It can bring retribution that in some cases can be quite devastating. "Blowing the whistle" and finding yourself unable to keep silent when you see a wrong may cost you your job, for instance.

    c.   Getting eaten becomes yet another witness. Share some historic examples from periods of Christian history where the risks were great and the sacrifices inspiring.

(You could use as an opening the humorous story of the person who, when fleeing from a lion, finally gave up and realized it was impossible to outrun the lion. The person knelt down to pray as the only recourse. When after a while the lion did not pounce, the person looked up and saw the lion also kneeling and praying. The person asked the lion, "What are you doing?" The lion replied, "Be quiet, please, I'm saying grace.")

A-5. A Drink At David's Place

Purpose Statement: *A communion sermon reflecting on the awesome responsibility we must feel at receiving the symbols of Jesus' dying for each one of us.*

1 Chronicles 11:15-19. David expresses a desire to have a drink of the delicious water from a well back home in Bethlehem. The problem is that the Philistines, with whom David is at war at the moment, occupy Bethlehem. Three of David's soldiers hear David's wish and fight their way through the Philistines to the well and bring a drink of water back to David. David was no doubt astounded over the feat and refuses to drink the water. Instead he pours it out on the ground as an offering to God, saying if he drank it, it would be like drinking the blood of the soldiers who risked their lives for the water.

Upon reflection, each of us might feel the same way regarding the symbols of Holy Communion that we are not worthy to receive that which was purchased at such a great price, or that we would be under an overwhelming obligation to Jesus if we did drink the cup and eat the bread of communion.

Then we remember Peter's reaction at the original Last Supper (John 13:2-9) when Jesus prepares to wash Peter's feet. He refuses to let Jesus serve him in this way and Jesus says that if Peter doesn't allow him to wash Peter's feet, "You will no longer be my disciple." Peter changes his attitude and asks Jesus to wash his hands and head as well as his feet.

Each of us needs to overcome our reluctance *really* to receive the symbols of this sacrament and commit ourselves to the responsibilities we assume when we receive the cup and the bread. It becomes an "offering to God," not poured out on the ground, but taken by us to nurture us for Christian service.

A-6. How Much Sin Is Too Much?

Purpose Statement: *If God always forgives our sins (when our repentance is real!), what does this mean for us, having this knowledge, while at the same time knowing we are about to willingly sin again?*

It seems to be a tricky position posing a tricky question. When we know we will be forgiven and yet we are contemplating our new sins with eagerness, it is like playing a game and drawing a card that reads, "You may have one free sin and bypass going to jail." Isn't this perilously close to Luther's criticism over the selling of indulgences?

There are some Christian fundamentalists (which some would claim to be an oxymoron) who assert that once you are saved, you can no longer sin again. A little rational thought quickly debunks such a notion. The most saintly of us find creative ways to sin every day. Consequently, how do we theologically maneuver around the problem of our future sins and their attendant forgiveness?

a. The Diminished Soul: The more we sin, the more our soul suffers shrinkage, and the less capable we become of differentiating right from wrong. Just as watching too much violence desensitizes us to violence, the more we sin the more desensitized we become to the problem. Another analogy would be: each additional drink taken by the social drinker renders that person less able to determine when to stop.

b. The Ingrained Habit: Obviously, the more we sin in general, or in particular harmful actions, the more it becomes habitual. The habit takes greater control of us making it more difficult even to repent.

c. The Receding Repentance: We begin to destroy our understanding of repentance and the nature of repentance. For example: Do we say to ourselves, "We may embezzle now, but we'll be honest later"? Are we telling God, "We don't love you now, but we will love you later"? We begin to think repentance is making a deal with God.

Some possible scriptures: Matthew 18:21-35; Matthew 5:29-30.

26

A-7. Don't Even Think It!

Purpose Statement: *We need to appreciate the fact that the thought is more dangerous than we imagine, and seek to discipline our thinking.*

(An alternative title might be "Perish The Thought!")

Matthew 5:27-30. It sounds as if Jesus is telling us that thinking about sin is just as bad as doing the actual deed. Our belief generally is that thinking about doing wrong is never as bad as actually putting our thoughts into actions. Occasionally, we might even talk ourselves into believing that as long as we don't carry through on the sin, simply thinking about it can't be harmful or wrong. However, Jesus often uses an enigmatic or inexplicable approach in order to make dramatic or emphatic some point that might otherwise be overlooked. He is simply concerned with our thoughts at the moment.

Of course, for all practical purposes, the deed is usually worse than the contemplation of it, especially for the victim. Each of us would prefer a mugger only to think about robbing us instead of actually robbing us. But Jesus is focusing for the time being on the perpetrator (each one of us). He might be saying that if you give yourself permission to do something wrong, but find yourself unable to carry out the plan, you are just as guilty as you would be if you actually followed through. In other words, you willed to do it and were prevented, not by moral conscience, but by inconvenience, fear, lack of opportunity, etc.

We are talking about the process whereby most good and bad actions come about. First we contemplate; then we entertain — we're tempted and finally act. This is the pattern of something beautiful such as falling in love, as well as something wicked like theft. What we spend our time dreaming about or dwelling upon can shape our disposition.

Somewhere I stumbled across this platitude:

> *Sow a thought — reap an act*
> *Sow an act — reap a habit*
> *Sow a habit — reap a character*
> *Sow a character — reap a destiny.*

A-8. Do You Know Our Secret Code?

Purpose Statement: *We need to know the meaning of the symbols of our church if they are to be relevant for us.*

Occasionally, we should be reminded of the explanation for each of our church symbols, which may include the sacraments (include the full seven of the Roman Catholic Church if you like, simply for educational purposes); the colors of the church year; the parts of the church (narthex, chancel, etc.); as well as the robe, hood, stoles, and academic colors; and, of course, the central symbols of cross, candles, ihs, ichthus, the image of the fish, etc.

  a. Start by giving a history of the need for symbols. The early church, under severe persecution, used symbols sometimes as a secret code, as in the image of the fish. The book of Revelation, according to theory, was written partly in code in order to survive in dangerous times so as to nurture Christians. There were long periods of history when many Christians could not read, and symbols on the walls and in stained glass were pictures to remind them of biblical stories and ideas.

  b. Hand out a page or have an insert filled with symbols and their explanations for a take-home piece.

  c. Close with the importance of our worship and the part that symbols play in helping us to focus on what it is that we are supposed to be doing in church.

For scripture, you could use a sample passage from Revelation illustrating the use of symbols as encouragement to our faith.

A-9. A Bunny Rabbit Church In A Tiger World

Purpose Statement: *The church needs to be more committed and disciplined if it expects to have a significant impact in this very tough world.*

Possible scriptures: Revelation 3:1-6, 14-17; Mark 13:9-13 among others you may select.

a. The world is rough and mean. It desperately needs help. There is too much suffering caused by people (aside from natural disasters).

b. One could argue the church is too soft. We are busy with sweet and lovely activities: birthday parties, choir exchanges, quilting, ice cream socials (all of which may be all right and serve some purpose). But are we engaging the real social and spiritual sources of evil in significant battle? The church has been directly and indirectly responsible for so much of the good in history: starting medical, educational, and various welfare agencies, as well as bringing a moral consciousness to all of our social progress. However, few of us today feel that the church is making anywhere near the contribution that an institution that calls itself "the body of Christ" should be making. We have taken on aspects of the world instead of impacting the world.

c. It is time for serious solutions.
   1. Get real and down to business.
   2. Set challenging goals. Churches might lose members if the church required more active participation in activities that called for sacrifice, change, and risk taking. How many Christians would be willing to go door-to-door talking with persons, or carry a picket sign in a demonstration?
   3. Assess the progress: success and failures. Presently, I don't believe that we honestly appreciate how far short we fall of our potential.

A-10. Were You Ever Somebody Else?

Purpose Statement: *Since church members may ask the question, it may be important for ministers to preach a sermon concerning the relationship of reincarnation to Christianity.*

Like ghosts and flying saucers, reincarnation is a topic that some of our church members enjoy speculating about. For some

Christians it may have captured the imagination since all of us ponder the mystery of death and what lies beyond this life. And "what happens to us after we die" is certainly central to our Christian faith.

I might suggest three comments on the issue:

a. There is no biblical evidence for reincarnation. It seems easy to deal with and dismiss the scripture passages which believers in reincarnation use to support their position. "You must be born again" (Jesus obviously meant spiritually in this life), the first Adam and second Adam reference, the second coming, Jesus as the second coming of Elijah (Luke 9:18-20), the transfiguration, and the man born blind (John 9:1-3) are all passages that have nothing to do with reincarnation, although they are used to support it.

b. There is certainly biblical evidence against reincarnation. Among the passages that preclude any possibility of reincarnation there is Paul's teaching about eternal life where the physical body becomes a spiritual body (1 Corinthians 15:35-58); Jesus' saying, "Today, you will be with me in paradise"; and all the stories assuming that you die and go to heaven (brothers marrying the widow, Dives and Lazarus, the Great Judgment, and so forth).

c. There are some logical ways reincarnation is opposed to Christian belief. Heaven as a place where loved ones are reunited is negated by the reincarnation belief that we move on to become other people without any remembered consciousness (that which makes us a consistent person). If nothing else, a continuation in an after-life we call heaven of those loving relationships that we begin in our lifetime here on earth is consistent with a loving God.

B.

B-1. Pursued By Whales?

Purpose Statement: *Does God have tasks for us that we are running away from?*

Using the story of Jonah we can examine some important possibilities concerning our responsibilities as Christians. Being a Christian means living a certain moral lifestyle of caring service. However, there may be, in addition, specific jobs we might feel God is calling us to.

a. How do we recognize God's calls? Do they always come in dramatic fashion like burning bushes or whales? Can God be calling us through quiet prayer, meditation, and evaluation of our talents, opportunities, and other means?

b. Are we trying to avoid those calls? Whether what we understand to be calls from God are actually that or not, many of us feel guilty that we may not be doing all that God expects of us as Christians because it will require doing something we won't like or making sacrifices we aren't ready to make.

c. Are we forced or pressured into responding? Jonah seems to have been unduly pressured to follow God's plan. Is it possible that not accepting a call from God will cause us to suffer some punishment? No, the author of Jonah is probably using exaggeration for dramatic effect. Our loving God would never threaten our freedom or force us into certain responses.

d. Will we be happy or unhappy if we accept? Yes and yes. Doing God's will can give us deep satisfaction and fulfillment. Doing God's will can also mean persecution and death (check out Bible and church history). Such hardship (except in very rare instances) is hardly likely, but we may not like our task or may be called to make uncomfortable sacrifices. However, the joy and spiritual growth, even in unpleasant circumstances, can be rewarding beyond measure.

B-2. Road Kill: Reducing People To So Many Rabbits

Purpose Statement: *Traffic deaths on our highways and streets are obscenely excessive and can be reduced significantly if Christians care enough to take the necessary steps.*

If we were serious about saving lives and avoiding automobile accidents, besides using seat belts, we would wear helmets and build our cars with crash bars over the top and around the front and sides. Race cars often crash at 200 miles an hour and the drivers walk away with just scratches! But this message is about slowing down. Speed kills! People debate the issue; however, it cannot be denied. If a deer runs out in front of your car, if your defective tires blow out, if you fall asleep, or any one of a number of possibilities, at slower speeds you have a greater chance of surviving an accident.

At our current speeds, statistics tell us that so many people will die on our streets and highways every year. And they will be sacrificed for our desire to get places faster. We put up with it because we really do have a philosophy of "it won't happen to us." For some reason we think we are special in God's eyes and God will protect our loved ones and us. If we were magically put in a situation where we could make a deal with God, promising never to drive over 45 miles per hour on the highways for the rest of our lives, and God guaranteeing that our daughter, brother, or any loved one would never be killed in an automobile accident, every one of us would take the deal.

A few years ago the speed limits were lowered nationwide and the death rate on our highways went down radically. However, the reason for lowering our speeds was to save gas and money, not lives. As it is now, we are told that slower drivers on the highways are the real danger. Like cattle we are forced to drive fast and keep

32

pace so as not to become obstacles, and in the process, we are sacrificing many lives.

If Christians cared, we would slow down and organize crusades to lower speed limits.

Scriptures that reflect Jesus' compassion for others could include Luke 13:34 and Matthew 9:35-38.

B-3. Is There A Lightning Bolt With Your Name On It?

Purpose Statement: *We must understand and eliminate the superstitions that control our lives in unhealthy ways.*

Aside from astrology, psychic readings, and other such nonsense, one serious superstition is the prominent belief that God steps into our lives and controls the "goings on" in ways that are very unGodlike. I find it very difficult to accept the implications of the incidents in Acts 5 where Ananias and Sapphira seem to have been struck down by God for deceit. Can we expect that of God today?

    a. Examples: Many believe that natural disasters such as floods and tornadoes are God's direct intervention to punish or warn us. A surprising number of people believe that "when your time comes, your time comes," and there is nothing you can do about it. A popular notion is that when a few people survive a bus crash that kills many others, God "had a reason to spare" them. Likewise, when a plane crashes and someone didn't arrive in time to make that flight, it is by God's design. Is this healthy theology?

    b. Problems: The idea prompted by narrowly missing disaster, that "someone up there must be watching over me," is popular because it is a comforting theology when coupled with the feeling most of us have that we are different and special and "it can't happen to us." God will take care of us. Thus God must have had very good reasons not to have taken care of the other folks who perished — reasons we

33

think probably won't be applicable to us in any near future. This kind of theology can do two unfortunate things:
1. It takes the logic and reason, the consistency and dependability out of our world. God can and, we trust, will step in and protect us. Nature and life are not understandable and constant. Natural laws cannot always be trusted.
2. This leads to irresponsibility. If there is "a time for each of us to go" in God's predestined plan, then we can feel more comfortable and secure and perhaps act more carelessly and irresponsibly.

c. Reality: Someone's missing a plane that later crashes, or being the lone survivor of a car accident, are not strange incidents or miracles. People miss flights where planes don't crash. A carton of eggs dropped to the floor may only break five out of the twelve. God works in our world through spiritual intervention — not through steering someone's hand at the wheel of his or her automobile to correct some foolish and dangerous mistake.

B-4. The Mark Of Cain Is On Us All!

Purpose Statement: *Since the mainline and major Christian denominations have all issued statements calling for the abolition of the death penalty, it is expected that the clergy would preach a sermon on the reasons why capital punishment is wrong.*

There are so many scriptures that are applicable: Matthew 5:38-48 and Romans 12:9-21 are powerful. Genesis 4 tells us that God marked Cain, a murderer, to protect him from the death penalty. Care must be taken not to mistake the dramatic pronouncement of God's revenge of seven lives as our permission to kill which misses the point of the "mark of Cain." There are so many reasons against the death penalty:
a. It does not deter crime. (There are plenty of good statistical studies for this.)

34

b. We are the only western industrialized ("civilized"?) nation still putting persons to death.
c. The progressive states abolished it. States with poorer education systems are more apt to have it.
d. Most mainline churches call for its abolition.
e. It is biased in practice. Usually, the poor and people of color have greater odds of being executed.
f. Believe it or not, the procedure to execute costs more than life-long incarceration. (However, putting a price tag on a life is wrong.)
g. It doesn't bring closure to the victims' families.
h. It hurts victims' families by giving them opportunities for revenge and physical expression of hate.
i. While the Old Testament permits it, the New Testament prohibits it.
j. Far too often history has proven that innocent people have been executed.
k. It is arbitrarily administered (location and pure chance are often deciding factors).
l. Given his nature of love and forgiveness, Jesus would never execute someone.

The only reason for capital punishment is to vent hate and revenge — which is anathema to the Christian faith.

B-5. Yes, God Does Take Attendance

Purpose Statement: *Though we can worship anywhere, any time, it is very important that Christians "go to church."*

Laypersons don't know that God requires ministers to take roll on Sunday mornings and turn in reports. It's time to tell them. Remind them that Jesus went to church regularly. Luke 2:41-49 (v. 42) in *Good News Version* uses the phrase "as usual" referring to Jesus' family's attendance, as does verse 16 in chapter 4 referring to Jesus' attendance. Jesus as a boy answered his parents by saying, "Didn't you know that I had to be in God's house?" Jesus attended church (synagogue) regularly despite his outspoken criticism of the religious institution and leaders.

There seems to be a rule in college that if the professor doesn't arrive within a certain time after the official starting time of the class (something on the order of ten minutes), the students may leave. They eagerly watch the clock and are overjoyed if they get the opportunity to miss class. Are we that way about church services? Will any excuse, no matter how insignificant, suffice to absent us from Sunday morning worship? It is very important that we attend church. Why?

- a. The church needs us. With all of its faults, still the church historically has been the greatest influence for moral behavior and the welfare of our communities of all other institutions. We, you and I, are the church.
- b. Others need us. One of our greatest oversights is failing to appreciate how important we, and our presence, are to other people at church. Just being there along with the love and support that we give to others is one of the most important things that happen all week. We are missed.
- c. We need it. Another of our greatest oversights is not realizing just how much the corporate worship and fellowship of other Christians can nurture our spirits.

B-6. If God Could Be Anybody She Wanted To Be, She'd Be Robin Hood

Purpose Statement: *We need to guard against greed and avarice, and have greater concern for the poor and disadvantaged.*

Given the biblical witness, and especially the teachings of Jesus, God has an inordinate concern with the corruption and sinfulness of having wealth, coupled with special attention to the poor. The philosophy of Robin Hood springs to mind. Somewhere a line has to be drawn for each person or family that establishes limits to permissible wealth. Anything in excess of such a limit, in a world filled with poverty and suffering, is disgraceful and immoral. What are those limits?

    a. What does the Bible have to say about wealth and poverty?

        1. Amos (2:6-8; 4:1-3), Jeremiah (5:26-29), Micah (2 and 6), and Isaiah (1:15-17), as exemplary of Old Testament teaching, were particularly hard on the wealthy.

        2. James 2:1-7 is indicative of the New Testament position.

        3. Remember how Jesus castigated the wealthy and supplicated for the poor in many dramatic teachings (the rich man and poor man who die; the statement concerning selling everything and giving to the poor; the poor widow putting her all in the offering; camels going through needles' eyes easier than going to heaven rich; etc.).

    b. How does that compare with the prevalent philosophy concerning possessions today?

        1. Athletes, CEOs, entertainment stars command outrageous incomes and then spend their money childishly.

        2. Greed runs rampant: one third-world dictator reportedly shipped $200 million in personal wealth into our country while our country was giving his country $250 million in aid.

        3. What used to be extravagant luxuries are now basic necessities.

    c. What does that have to do with us?

        1. Are we just as greedy as the super wealthy, but we just don't have the same opportunities to get it and waste it?

        2. Do we dream of wealth — buy lottery tickets to win millions?

        3. Perhaps most of us are too wealthy now.

B-7. What's The Matter With Sex?

Purpose Statement: *A sermon intended to help the Christian find a healthier attitude concerning sexuality.*

After creating everything God thought it was all "good," or as another translation would put it, God "was pleased" with creation. Somehow, we have a tendency to associate "the fall" of Adam and Eve with sex. Lurking in the background (not too far back) is the notion that they were innocent and only when they became sexually aware and active did they become knowledgeable and sinful. Genesis 2:21-25 tells us that they were not embarrassed over their nakedness at that time, but later on they felt compelled to hide from God because they were ashamed of their nakedness. Yet today we associate modesty with embarrassment and shame. Our nakedness is somehow immoral, offensive, and impure. I'm not suggesting that our society become one large nudist colony. I am suggesting that we see our bodies and human sexuality as beautiful and good.

a. Often sex is seen as negative and associated with connotations of "dirty," wicked, and sinful.
1. The media has had its part in making sex a "seamy" business.
2. The church contributes to our common cultural attitude. Some clergy are denied marriage as are also nuns who are held to be of a high and lofty order. The Roman Catholic theologian Schillebeeckx doesn't try to cover up the fact that it is because the church sees sex as not pure. Paul says it is better to remain single.

b. God intends sex to be beautiful and good.
1. The church has always been torn between the opposites of aestheticism (the world is beautiful and good, and meant to be enjoyed) and asceticism (the world is bad and we should forego physical and fleshly pleasures for the spiritual).
2. We must return to the attitude expressed in the Genesis account of God's creation that the body and all its parts

are good and sex is beautiful — unless we distort it. It is by sex that we become partners with God as co-creators.

B-8. Mystery Of The Red Dragon

Purpose Statement: *This is an opportunity to preach on apocalyptic literature in our Bible and the ways it is abused and misunderstood.*

Begin the message with a little education on apocalyptic material in Revelation, Daniel, Mark 13, 2 Thessalonians 2, (Enoch), and so forth. Revelation 12 and its story of the red dragon could be used to illustrate the difficulty of apocalyptic literature. This kind of material has two central themes:

    a. Christians must remain strong and trust God in times of persecution or trouble. Explain the purpose for the cryptic language and strange symbols found in apocalyptic material. It should be made clear that we don't fully understand all of the references indicated by the beasts, numbers, visions, and strange language. We must avoid the many preachers and books purporting to have the answers: the bear is Russia, etc. The fact is no one has unraveled the confusion. The mystery of the red dragon has not been solved. We must simply search the material to glean out any clear passages of encouragement to keep our faith strong and ignore the rest.

    b. Jesus is returning soon. Paul finally warned people to stop dwelling on this issue, and Jesus said we not only can't know the time, but it is a "wicked generation who looks for signs." It is foolish and a waste of time to try to anticipate a second coming of Jesus. It shouldn't matter if it happens today, fifty years from now, or never. We should be living the Christian life regardless of any return date. If we are living the Christian life only because Jesus may come tomorrow, then our reason is selfish and our life phony. If we needed a sense of urgency to "get us saved" and frighten us into a "conversion," our imminent death should do that. We could die any moment and that possibility is far more probable than the second coming this week.

(see sermon B-10)

B-9. Do We Have To Like Going To Church?

Purpose Statement: *While there are "parts" of going to church that are not meant to be enjoyed, we should be growing in our appreciation and deep satisfaction connected with church going.*

I have two answers to the question, "Do we have to like going to church?" The first answer is an emphatic, "No!" And the second answer is an equally emphatic, "Yes!" And I do not believe that they are contradictory.

a. No. There should be considerable elements to the church experience that we find uncomfortable and even distasteful. Unless we are perfect already, at times we should be disturbed by the kinds of challenges confronting us from sermons, classes, and discussion groups in church. There are certain areas of our lives that need change that will perhaps require serious sacrifices. These may involve, or be initiated by, a deep remorse and repentance over ways we have offended others. Other challenges may be in the order of commitments to serve in unpleasant ways, or requests to dig deeper into our pockets. We may or may not enjoy our employment or school, and yet these are important and necessary activities. Chances are we will not like going to the hospital, but again, it is important and extremely helpful.

b. Yes. In this day and age we tend to be entertainment oriented. Leisure time activities, television, movies, sports, and so forth condition us to seek good times and amusement. We begin to measure church with entertainment activities and develop inappropriate expectations.

However, there is much satisfaction, if not even some fun, to be had in the life of the church. There should be:

- enjoyment in learning and growing in church,
- inspiration in worship,
- satisfaction in serving, and
- joy in fellowship.

It pretty much depends on our attitudes and expectations. If we give ourselves to what the Christian Church is all about, there are great rewards and joy to be had.

B-10. Is There Any Future In The Bible?

Purpose Statement: *It is important to preach on the nature of biblical prophecy to dispel the myths and false notions so many Christians have concerning this subject and allowing them to find the special values in the prophetic tradition.*

    a. What we sometimes think prophecy is. We mistakenly think that biblical prophecy is mainly predicting the future. This would mean that there is a certain predestination concerning human events, a notion that we shed long ago. Evangelical Christians have a tendency to waste too much time on efforts to find out when "the end" is coming. This, despite the fact that Jesus said no one knows the time (Matthew 24:36). How can the fundamentalists ignore this passage along with the statement in verse 44 that the second coming would be when we are not expecting it? Then, wouldn't the expectations of the conservatives negate the second coming? God is not playing silly games with us by hiding secret numbers and symbols in scripture to make a scavenger hunt for us. We play the game by picking out certain "signs" that seem relevant and ignoring the others. This, in the light of Jesus' saying that it is an evil generation that looks for signs. It would seem very egocentric of us to believe that the entire message of a second coming

41

applies to us after skipping over all the previous generations. But then the idea is self-centered anyway: is it very honest to "be good" because Mommy and Daddy are coming home, or because that is just our real character?

b. What biblical prophecy really is. Perhaps two central thoughts can be found in prophecy. First, a messiah will come some day to save the people. This message is found only in very vague and general terms, no specifics. Second, Amos, Jeremiah, Hosea, Isaiah, etc. were simply telling the people to "shape up" and start living as God wants them to or there would be dire consequences.

c. What's in it for us? We can glean the biblical prophecy for inspiration to live more courageously and faithfully. Use any scripture from the prophets listed above or others that challenge us to stop living greedily and selfishly.

(see sermon B-8)

C.

C-1. What On Earth Is God Doing?

Purpose Statement: *Every pastor must preach on the question that, sooner or later, every Christian must ask, "Why did God create a world where there is so much sin and pain?"*

Many ministers believe that the only good answer to this question is the answer the book of Job finally arrives at: "We can't know the mysterious ways of God." But there are some logical reasons why God built a world where evil and pain are not only possible, but also necessary. First, it is my belief that God does not do evil things: Matthew 7:9-11 and James 1:12-18 are appropriate scriptures. However, I would emphasize three thoughts:

    a. Pain is necessary.
        1. The world needs contrasts: we can't have up without down, or cold without hot, or good without bad, or comfort without pain.
        2. Struggle against trouble and disasters causes us to grow as individuals and as a race.
    b. Sin is necessary.
        1. Freedom requires the opportunity to do good and *evil.*
        2. Without freedom, we would be puppets or robots and not real humans.
        3. To have a social world, that freedom allows us to hurt and help others.
    c. God doesn't fail us.
        1. God provides strength in trouble as attested to in the faith of the martyrs.
        2. Eternal life or heaven makes all the suffering and wrongs in this life pale into insignificance. (A child deprived of something it wants badly sees it as a tragedy. But later, as an adult, it will understand how unimportant it really was at the time.)

(Humorous story: A person stranded on the roof of the house in a flood, replied repeatedly to those who came to rescue [a rowboat, a motorboat, and a helicopter], "God will save me." When the person died in the flood and went to heaven, the first thing the person did was to ask God why God didn't come to the rescue. God answered, "I can't imagine what went wrong. I sent two boats and a helicopter.")

C-2. Do You Know What You Are Drinking?

Purpose Statement: *We need to be reminded every so often of the commitment we should be making when we receive Holy Communion.*

Given the nature of Communion, care should be given to explain to children some rudiments of this activity so as to avert any strange notions they could develop. However the thoughts of this message are for adults who become too familiar with this sacrament and so forget the significance of their act of receiving the bread and the cup.

Matthew 26:39: Jesus asked if it was possible to have "this cup pass," meaning that he did not want to die on the cross. Matthew 26:27: at the Last Supper he asked all of his disciples to drink from the cup. Matthew 20:20-23: Mrs. Zebedee asks a special favor for her sons and Jesus asks if they can "drink from the cup" that he was about to drink (suffer and die), and they answer, "We can." Jesus agrees that they indeed will. One must assume that when we drink from the cup we should be making a commitment of loyalty to the teachings of Jesus as faithful followers. This may mean serious sacrifice. This theme could be developed in such a way:

   a. What Jesus did for us by accepting the cup.
   b. What we are promising when we receive the cup.
   c. What are some of the possible consequences for us?

Two hymns that seem so appropriate are "Are Ye Able, Said The Master" and "Fill My Cup, Lord."

C-3. Christians Should Be Different — Not Weird

Purpose statement: *The title says it all: there is a happy medium for the Christian between being no different from everyone else and being strange enough so others cannot relate to us.*

Elijah, Elisha, Jeremiah, Ezekiel, John the Baptist were different. In contrast, Jesus seemed very normal. The nature of religion has attracted some "far out" people and ideas since Bible times: snake handling, refusing medical help, Mormon polygamy, witch burning, "treeing the devil" (Cane Ridge, Kentucky, 1801: 25,000 people listened to five preachers at the same time and many of them barked like dogs — the people, not the preachers), groups that permit no sex, the end of the world folks, "rebirthing therapy sessions" (that have caused death), devil worshipers, and those who abstain from all modern conveniences (cars, phones, electricity, etc.), to name a few.

While not intentionally trying to separate ourselves from other folks as being better than they are, yet we cannot be totally indistinguishable from the masses. There should be enough evidence to recognize us as Christians if our faith means anything. Christians should be different in:

a. Our witness. Coming on with a blunt, "Are you saved?" or "Do you know Jesus Christ as your personal savior?" is one sure way to send a prospect running. We witness to our faith through our exemplary behavior as good loving citizens and yet without being ostentatious.

b. Our ethics. We don't cheat on our taxes or steal "little" things from work because "everyone is doing it" or it won't be missed. There is a good chance that we will even be misunderstood for our ethical stands.

c. Our love. If our moral stands seem to keep some people at arm's length because they are uncomfortable around us, our love, warmth, eagerness to serve and help, our honesty, our humility, and our understanding should be an attraction.

45

John 17:14-16, Romans 12:2, and 1 Corinthians 1:18-21 would be appropriate scriptures.

Realistically, usually our greatest danger is not being different enough rather than being too different.

C-4. Forgive Us Our Daily Bread

Purpose Statement: *As an especially privileged nation, we are a notoriously overfed population, which leads to the usual sins associated with luxury.*

Luke 16:19-31 is excellent and Amos 4:1-3 is poignant regarding overeating and neglect of the hungry. The introduction could commence with facts and figures on the world's hungry, including those in our own communities.

After a statement concerning how there is nothing wrong about enjoying good food, for the following reasons we need to ask God to forgive us our daily bread because:

a. We too often take our food abundance for granted.
b. We waste food. At restaurants, church dinners, banquets, etc., I look around and am appalled at how often people leave most of the food on their plates. I wonder how we got to be so overweight. My wife says, "They eat junk food at home."
c. We eat too much. We are jeopardizing our health with how much we eat, as well as what we eat.
d. We forget the starving.
e. We *try* to forget the starving.
f. We "get tired of hearing about the starving." This is one thing a Christian cannot afford to do: get tired of hearing about anyone in need.

C-5. Sticks And Stones — But Mostly Names

Purpose Statement: *A sermon on differentiating insults from nick-names and good-natured kidding.*

It seems there is a fine line between friendly teasing and words that hurt. Christians should be more sensitive than other people about words or phrases that can offend other people. Our sensitivity has been heightened in recent times by concern over racism and being "politically correct." It isn't always easy to know what is in good taste and what goes beyond what is appropriate. Jesus called Peter, "Satan"; he called Herod, that "old fox"; he called the religious leaders hypocrites and other bad names; and he appeared to call a woman who came to him for help, a "dog." Perhaps there are at least three guidelines we could use:

a. Some comments are obviously offensive and should never be used. Racial slurs are not appropriate under any circumstances. Fortunately we are becoming more sensitized concerning inappropriate language today: "blackmail" should be "extortion," "low man on the totem pole" should be something like "person not given much respect," and so forth.

b. When you know the person very well, perhaps are very good friends, you probably occasionally use intimate names such as "Tiny" for an overweight friend or "Curly" for a person with little hair. Even then, it would pay to rethink the situation. Does the friend respond to the nickname to cover hidden feelings? Teasing friends is usually a sign of a feeling of not only intimacy, but also popular regard. One must be careful of the kidding and joking! Some mischievous boys called the prophet, Elisha, "baldy" (2 Kings 2:23-24). He promptly called two bears out of the woods and had them eat the 42 boys.

c. Is it appropriate to join in even when the person selects his or her own nicknames or jokes about some feature such as being bald or overweight? It might be wise to visit with them tactfully before joining in their use of unflattering terms.

An incident of extraordinary sensitivity is the story of Jesus sensing the light touch of the woman in the crowd (Mark 5:25-34). His disciples (v. 31) couldn't believe he could feel one person's slight contact when many were pressing around him.

C-6. Mistaking Santa Claus For God

Purpose Statement: *We need to continue to grow in our understanding of God.*

Another title could be "Yes, Virginia, There Is a God (or Jesus)." Santa Claus and Jesus share a special day and the two could be easily confused as well as could God and Santa Claus.
  a. Similarities between God and Santa Claus:
     1. Both are mystical and never seen (Santa Claus only a short time before Christmas).
     2. Both are capable of the miraculous.
     3. Both see all and know all.
     4. Both seem to have two lists, one good and one bad.
     5. Both reward us for being good.
     6. Both are stereotypically viewed as old men with long white hair and beard.
  b. Dangers in mistaking God for Santa Claus:
     1. Commercialism.
     2. Greed.
     3. Emphasis on receiving physical gifts.
     4. God may begin to seem unreal.
     5. For some there is a tendency to "outgrow" God and leave religion for the children.
  c. Qualities unique to God:
     1. Unconditional love.
     2. Amazing forgiveness.
     3. Total relevancy to every aspect of life.
     4. The gift of salvation.
  Scripture: One of the Christmas stories from Matthew or Luke, or Revelation 20:11-15.

C-7. Is It Time For Another Flood?

Purpose Statement: *We need to consider the critical question: "What is the human condition?"*

Just how bad is our world? Are we too greedy, violent, apathetic, insensitive, wasteful, hateful, selfish, etc.? What direction are we going? Is the world improving or getting worse? What can we do about it?

a. Thesis: The world is a beautiful and wonderful place full of potential for great joy and love. God created a paradise and "saw that it was good." Some souls are optimistic and see the world as improving despite all of the trouble and suffering. They see "some good in each individual." That, if it could only be cultivated, each person would be a good, kind citizen.

b. Antithesis: There seems plenty of reasons to be pessimistic: several wars going on constantly around the globe, too much crime and violence, domestic abuse and family failures, people starving by the millions. Reading the daily newspaper can be a depressing experience. The flood myth exemplifies the pessimist philosophy. God became so unhappy with our behavior that it seemed best to destroy the world and start over (Genesis 6:5-8). *The Lord of the Flies* was a twentieth century parable asking the question, "Just how far removed from the animals or savage behavior are we?"

c. Synthesis: Perhaps the first step towards a solution is to begin with self-improvement. Luke 6:37-42 is a powerful passage concerning the logs and specks in our eyes and where to start the healing process. 1) Do we have a herd mentality or do we think for ourselves? 2) Are we insecure or do we have a healthy attitude? 3) Do we hate too much or are we compassionate? 4) Are we greedy and selfish or are we generous and thoughtful? We are all a composite of good and bad and have sufficient room for improvement.

49

C-8. The Trick Is To Hear The Rooster Before

Purpose Statement: *Because we forget some of our Christian obligations until too late, we need ways to remind ourselves to be alert and diligent about the Christian business.*

Luke 22:31-34, 54-62. We all know the familiar story of Peter denying Jesus and then being reminded by the rooster crowing.

a. The problem: Hindsight is too late. They say experience teaches, but it teaches too late. Actually that isn't entirely true as far as future events go. However, it is very true regarding the current event from which the lesson is derived. After the situation is passed we ask ourselves, "Why did I do that? Why didn't I think before saying or doing that?" As an example, how many of us get angry in traffic when we believe someone has been rude to us or has placed us in danger, and display road rage. Then, later (!), we hear the rooster crow. This may be a very common ailment.

b. The solution: Get prepared. The Boy Scouts have a motto that should be a prime Christian tenet: "Be prepared." Since we cannot predict coming events, we need to anticipate possibilities.

1. At the beginning of each day, go through a ritual of reminding ourselves that anything could happen: some person with a very unpleasant disfigurement may pop up and you could be caught staring; someone could insult you and you should be ready to make a kind response; an opportunity to help or serve another person could occur instantly. Anticipate strange occurrences at the beginning of each day and you will respond more appropriately.

2. Practice pretending that Jesus is with you and you are showing him around your community. In his presence, you should be on your best behavior.

3. Develop your own roosters or reminders. These would be symbols such a cross on your ring or around your neck, a sign on the wall, a little statue on your desk, etc.

50

The difficulty is that these become routine and so common as to soon be overlooked. They need replacing regularly with some other roosters.

C-9. I Hope Our New Earth Gets Done On Time

Purpose Statement: *It is the Christian pastor's obligation to preach periodically on ecology and the good stewardship of our environment.*

Scripture: Psalm 8 (the wonder of God's magnificent creation and our place of responsibility), Genesis 1 and 2 (the creation and the garden of paradise), Hosea 4:1-3 (no love in the land and the land and animals will die), Revelation 21:1-4 (a new heaven and a new earth).

    a. Devastation. There are so many statistics available to sensitize us dramatically to the destruction of our environment: air and water pollution, depletion of natural resources (forests, oil, ozone layer, and minerals), erosion of land, paving over productive land, the waste in throw-away products for land fill, etc.

    b. Reflection. We should continually remind ourselves of the need to be good stewards of this earth, which is a gift from God. We are rapidly moving towards destroying the planet for our descendents and ourselves. Taking good care of our environment is sound theology.

    c. Restoration. Present a list of ways to become good citizens and stewards environmentally.

       1. Recycle.

       2. Bus, bicycle, or walk whenever possible.

       3. Don't litter or waste.

       4. Conserve power and water.

       5. Join an effective conservation group.

       6. Keep legislators informed.

       7. (Plus many other possibilities)

Somewhere I read that it costs $80 million a day to have clean water in our world while we spend $240 million each day on cigarettes and almost one and a half billion dollars on war weapons.

C-10. Why Teachers Can't Pray

Purpose Statement: *It is important to preach a clarification sermon on the issue of Bible reading and prayer in the public schools.*

This sometimes very hot issue is not going away soon and too many of our church members do not understand what is involved. They believe that it is normal and appropriate to have Bible reading and prayer in the public schools and because it is not allowed, this is one of the big sources of the problems with teens today. There are many good points that could be used in this sermon, a few of which follow:

a. It is important to give a good history of past incidents of corruption when the Christian Church and the government have been in collusion. Many European countries provide classic examples.

b. Give the legal reasons why there needs to be a separation between Church and State.

c. Emphasize the need for Christians to play fair and to not take advantage of being in the majority. We shouldn't be practicing our religion in public institutions supported by tax money when other religions cannot. (I don't want my children worshiping as Muslims or Hindus in public schools, and people of other faiths feel the same about Christianity.)

d. Excusing atheists or people of other faiths during "religious exercises" in public schools discriminates and singles them out as strange or different.

e. Such religious activity is inappropriate, becoming, sometimes, a show (Matthew 6:1) and, sometimes, common and "watered down" to insignificance. Christian witness should be practiced by how we live and who we are, and not through taking advantage of tax-supported "captured" audiences.

f.   Prayer and Bible reading are not prohibited in public schools. But it should remain an individual experience and not organized by the state. Any teacher or student wishing to pray or read the Bible in spare time is free to exercise his or her faith as long as it does not infringe on the time of others.

Besides Matthew 6, Mark 12:13-17 is a helpful passage concerning certain responsibilities belong to the Church and others to the State.

D.

D-1. Don't Fight, Don't Run — What's Left?

Purpose Statement: *We need constant reminders always to seek peaceful or nonviolent solutions to confrontations.*

Given the social nature of our world and its continuingly more crowded condition, conflicts and violent situations will arise. How prepared are we to defuse volatile moments and change anger or hate into amicable feelings? Jesus preached peace and love constantly. Matthew 26:47-53 gave instructions to "put up your sword." Luke 6:27-36 counseled a turning of the other cheek. Similar passages are legion.

    a. The taboo. Vengeance is wrong. Violence brings revenge and revenge brings hate and counter-revenge. There can be no war to end all wars. You cannot "get even." Someone is always behind and needs retaliation.

    b. The method. 1) Sometimes fighting is appropriate; remember Jesus in the Temple angry with the moneychangers. 2) Running can be timely; remember Jesus left the city earlier in Holy Week to avoid being captured. Knowing when these options are best is difficult and takes practice and prayer. 3) The main alternative and most dominant response remains pacifism: reason, love, reconciliation, forgiveness, kindness, and even sacrificing to help an "enemy." We are woefully ignorant about the many, many successful examples of pacifism, both personal and international, in our history. Search out these examples to share in this sermon.

    c. The rules. 1) Don't hurt another, either physically or by insult. 2) Always use love and kindness. 3) Make the goal reconciliation. 4) Seek intentional goodwill towards the "enemy."

    d. Some hints. 1) Study and pray continually over the love and peace teachings of Jesus. 2) Practice remembering, "I am a Christian and must strive to be like Jesus." 3) Prepare before leaving home to anticipate what situations could arise and plan how you will respond.

Jesus was brutally abused and killed and yet with love asked forgiveness for his attackers. That act of love brought us here today!

D-2. The Proper Way To Wear A Halo

Purpose Statement: *A sermon seems necessary occasionally on the fine line we have to tread between improper witnessing and evangelism, and the other extreme of none at all.*

Basic to our understanding of appropriate witnessing is the juxtaposition of two important scriptures: Matthew 5:14-16 concerning our being the light of the world and Matthew 6:1 concerning doing our piety in front of others. There would seem to be three positions: the right way, the wrong way, and no way at all. Too many of us err on the side of no way at all. We may find it uncomfortable or embarrassing to witness for our faith, or simply feel confused about how to do it.

   a. Wrong way. Everybody acknowledges that we are to let our light shine. However, Jesus has cautioned us against becoming too self-righteous, and parading our "goodness" to impress others for self-aggrandizement. How many people have been driven away from Christianity because their contact has been with the "goody-goodies" or the phonies and hypocrites. When I hear too much "God talk" ("Praise the Lord," "Thank you, Jesus," or "God must have a reason"), I find myself wanting to back away. I find the posture of "You need to be like me, I've found the Lord" somewhat unsettling. We shouldn't need to tell others how good we are. Remember the quote, "What you are speaks so loud I can't hear what you say"? Jesus makes a long and scathing attack on the religious folk in chapter 23 of Matthew. I once heard an overly pious woman say to a group that included a person whose eyes were very discolored by blindness, "The eyes are the windows of the soul. You can look into a person's eyes and see if they are filled with the Spirit."

b. Right way. We must never mistake "personality" for the presence of the Holy Spirit. Unfortunately, some bubbly, Christian extroverts are assumed to be more spiritual than the silent types. Enthusiasm and silence alike may accompany those who are truly the light of the world. However, one characteristic should always be present — humility. Instead of the pose, "You need to find Christ and become *like me*," we need to share the attitude of, "We are both sinners needing to join the faith struggle hand in hand." Jesus gave excellent examples such as: the Pharisee and sinner in the Temple (Luke 18:9-14) and where to sit when invited to dinner (Luke 14:7-11). Our best and real witness is in being a loving and caring person. If people feel comfortable around us, trust us, and know they can come to us for understanding and help, we are witnessing in a meaningful way.

D-3. Turn 'Em In — That's What Friends Are For

Purpose Statement: *There is a time to break confidences or to betray secrets in order to help persons.*

We are raised to believe that being a squealer or a snitch, and tattling or ratting out are wrong. Some persons would consider it one of the lowest forms of sin. However, with some objective observations we could be led to understand it as a virtue in many instances.

a. What? We are dealing with occasions where we break confidences or seemingly betray a trust. There are two classic examples in scripture. 1 Samuel 20 tells the story of Jonathan taking confidences from his father, Saul, to David. One could say Jonathan betrayed his father in telling David things Saul did not want David to know. Another dramatic example is Rahab, a resident of Jericho, turning traitor to her city and betraying it to Joshua in order for Joshua to capture the city (Joshua 2). In both cases, these people could be said to be disloyal. We as adults, and many times children, have opportunities to choose between keeping a secret and squealing. Sometimes squealing is the proper road to take.

b. Why? The addict or alcoholic we turn in will find greater help in the long run. Youth may be doing friends a favor, even it they don't appreciate it, by referring them to authorities (say, for inhaling mood-altering substances) to prevent dangerous behavior. Crime stoppers are good. Even a counselor should betray a confession or confidence if the person is dangerous to her or himself or to others. In many cases the person we turn in may not understand that we have actually done him the highest good. He may always hate us.

c. When? We always need criteria to evaluate a situation in order to determine the proper course. It isn't always easy, but we have to make decisions. In most of the kinds of situations we are talking about there are only two avenues. You cannot abstain or remain neutral. The old adage, "Not to decide is to decide," is never truer than in these cases. Our criteria will be selecting the higher good in a clash of principles. The principles are keeping a confidence or secret on the one hand, and perhaps bringing about a greater good to the party involved or to other innocent potential victims. The latter course may be called for.

D-4. Why I Am Not A Fundamentalist

Purpose Statement: *Each church member should know enough about different Christian theologies to be able to make intelligent choices regarding churches, beliefs, activities, and issues.*

A continuum is a line or string of increments denoting relationships — oftentimes with two poles or extreme opposites: hot/cold, up/down, good/evil, etc. (This is my definition, not a dictionary one.) There is a strong tendency for theology to fall out into a continuum between, let us say, two poles that might be labeled liberalism and fundamentalism. We must be cautious about labeling persons and be very much aware that most of us are inconsistent enough to be neatly compartmentalized. A strong case can be made for such a continuum of theological thought and conservative, neo-orthodox, etc. theologies tend to line up along that continuum. The following reasons might suffice why a mainline Christian would shun fundamentalism:

a. A fundamentalist believes he or she has a corner on the truth. They are right and you are wrong. A liberal tends to say we are all still struggling to find the truth and everyone possesses some of it (1 Corinthians 13:12).

b. A fundamentalist's God is cruel: ordering "chosen people" to kill others (as in the Old Testament), and assigning otherwise good people to an eternal torture for not believing in Jesus. They blame God for terrible things that happen ("God had a reason"). They seem to have missed out on Jesus' teachings of a loving God or the many passages such as 1 John 4:7-21 or Matthew 7:9-11.

c. The fundamentalist's major concern seems to be the egocentric need to "get saved" and the message to you is the self-oriented "Get yourself saved." The liberal's theme is usually one of caring for and serving others (Matthew 25:31-40).

D-5. Why Did God Hide Heaven?

Purpose Statement: *A good sermon on why God hasn't given us more information concerning heaven might interest more than a few church members.*

   a. Some concept of heaven is central to the Christian faith. Without some existence beyond this life, the injustices, pain, and suffering of this life would make this world a cruel and obscene joke. Some sinners live long and prosperous lives while some innocent children starve to death after a brief twelve or fifteen years of misery. Some form of afterlife is necessary if there is a just and loving God.
   b. Yet it remains obscure and mysterious. We know so much about this life and our world that in contrast, heaven remains a vague shadow. It is so well hidden from us that we are often prone to doubts and question its existence.
   c. There must be good explanations.
      1. One obvious reason we cannot know very much is that we are told it is a spiritual world. Paul said our physical bodies must put on the spiritual to experience heaven. We are so enmeshed in the physical we find it difficult to sense the spiritual to any extent.
      2. If heaven were made more real to us, it would become a bribe. We would be so convinced of its reality and nature that we would strive to "be good" for the sole reason of getting to heaven. An analogy could be how we might "kow-tow" to a rich aunt to secure a significant place in her will. It is just vague enough to be out of reach of temptation. Our love for other people must remain our motivation for ethical behavior.
      3. Matthew 13:10-17 speaks to the vagueness of heaven and Jesus gives us a partial explanation. He says that the more we are in tune with him, the better sense we have of heaven. If we ask, seek and knock, or study Jesus thoroughly, the more we begin to understand about what the afterlife must be like. Beyond that it must remain clothed in mystery.

D-6. Birds Of A Feather ... Become Xenophobic

Purpose Statement: *Racism and the related "we versus them" phenomena are still serious diseases in society and need to be addressed regularly in sermons.*

Galatians 3:26-28 is such a beautiful passage connoting our oneness in Christ because we are all sisters and brothers as children of God. This doesn't mean we don't recognize and thoroughly appreciate diversity. It means we enjoy it and never let it become in any way divisive! Unfortunately, there is a serious discrepancy between the ideal of this scripture and reality. Our world is torn apart by divisiveness and dissension caused by our tendency to collect in groups of similarities and shun those we perceive as different in some way. This is the cause of wars, as well as altercations of a milder nature. One possible way to attack the issue might be the following three points.

    a. Examples. Start by presenting numerous illustrations of "we versus them" such as: racism, skinheads, states arguing over water rights in a river, people worrying over other states getting "our money" because we don't have gambling and "our people" are taking their money elsewhere, and "buying American." Some people who refuse to buy "foreign" cars are ignorant of the fact that many parts of "American" cars are built in other countries, while some "foreign" cars are made in the United States. We worry about the Japanese buying up property in our country and are in no way concerned that Britain owns more than the Japanese. It makes a difference if they look like us! (An excellence resource is *Buying Into America* by Martin and Susan Tolchin, published by Times Books.)

    b. Reasons. We fear what seems different. We are ignorant of facts. We need someone lower on the social or ethical ladder to make ourselves look better. We need group identification and to band together against a common "enemy."

    c. Solutions. We must educate ourselves concerning the problem. The subtleties of the issue are enormous. Rivalries in school sports are too serious. Different religious groups can't cooperate. Even flying the American flag is making a statement of "we versus them!" We must immerse ourselves in diversity appreciation experiences! Galatians 3:26-28 is our goal.

D-7. Does God Believe In Astrology And Flying Saucers?

Purpose Statement: *Superstitions are plagues that we must eradicate.*

Werewolves and vampires don't exist, but superstitions do. And they consume our time, our energy, and sometimes our money. They frighten us, confuse us, and lead us astray. Among them (ghosts, astrology, witches, flying saucers, and religious superstitions) some are harmless and fun to speculate about, while others are misleading and harmful. I will place them in three categories. The Old Testament puts together three superstitions (one from each of my categories) in an interesting passage from 1 Samuel 28:3-15 — a fortuneteller or witch, a ghost, and perhaps some religious superstition.

a. The "no ways." Examples of superstitions that have no validity and deserve no respect would include witches, fortune-tellers, mediums, and astrology. These are all phony and are used to take advantage of the unwary. Some may even take your money. The people of Salem did atrocious things because they believed in witches. Today people waste time with the foolishness of astrology. Ever notice how horoscopes limit their "predictions" to just common sense suggestions ("Today is a good day to be careful.")? The concocters of these silly prognostications realize they must be careful about the advice they give so as to avoid lawsuits.

b. The "maybes." I don't believe in ghosts and flying saucers; they seem far too improbable. Yet, I will not ridicule those who do believe. No one can with absolute assurance say they don't exist. So, until more evidence is forthcoming, they are just fun to talk about.

c. The "must get over its." The most damaging superstitions would have to be theological. Too many Christians believe things about God and the Bible that are misleading, confusing, and irresponsible. Examples would include: "God had a reason for sending a flood to a specific community," or "Every word of the Bible is true" (which leads to unfortunate behavior such as capital punishment and vengeance), or "When your time comes...." Religious superstitions need to be dealt with in a serious manner as they lead to belief in a cruel God, discrimination towards others, and personal carelessness.

D-8. Moved Any Mountains Lately?

Purpose Statement: *Should we be able to heal people with prayer, and if so what can we heal?*

We've heard of various faith healers, some of whom are even on television. Should we believe in them? Some Christians (Christian Scientists) believe so much in prayer that they disapprove of any medical practice. How do we feel about healing prayer? Do we expect it to happen? Has it happened for us? A mother of a very sick boy read about a tree where the face of Jesus was purported to have been seen. She was taking him to the tree, believing that if he touched the tree, he would be healed. We realistically know that a great many of our prayers for healing have not been efficacious. We ask why. Luke 9:1-6 records Jesus having given the disciples the power to heal. Shouldn't we be able to heal like them?

a. Some healing prayers have worked. We know that. Whether psychosomatic or God's healing, or at different times both, we believe that prayer will heal.

b. Most of us believe that we can't heal everything. Since biblical days no prayer has raised the dead, the ultimate healing. Prayer does not grow back an arm that has been lost. The best faith healers and Christians Scientists have failures. And we know of so many incidents where prayer didn't heal. So sometimes we can and sometimes we can't.

c. When we fail, is it the sick person's fault? Mark 10:46-52 tells the story of blind Bartimaeus being healed because he had faith. Should we assume that when prayer doesn't heal it is because the sick one did not believe? That may be beyond our power to know. However, we must remember we cannot heal all diseases or injuries.

d. Could it all hinge on our faith? Mark 11:22-25 is a remarkable statement by Jesus. We are told that, if we believe, anything we pray for we will receive. By prayer, we can move mountains into the sea. Again we are confronted by Jesus' style of exaggeration in order to make a point. Just believing is not enough; Jesus would also add that it must be in harmony with God's will. The concept of needing to believe if it is to happen has its tricky side also. How are we able to believe it will happen if we know that not everything we pray for is going to happen or can happen? And, supposedly, if we don't believe and have faith, it won't happen. Perhaps someone else has an answer to this conundrum. If so, please write.

e. Finally, God's will must take precedence. Even Jesus in the garden during the closing moments of his life prayed not to have to go to the cross, but acquiesced to God's will. We believe in prayer, that it is answered sometimes, and that God wants us to be whole and healthy. We can ask for no more.

D-9. Table Manners

Purpose Statement: *Most of us become too casual and complacent at the Communion table.*

Paul reminds us (1 Corinthians 11:17-34) that it is possible to forget the significance of Holy Communion and come to the table carelessly. We know that it is more than possible; some do it regularly. Verses 28 and 29 speak directly to the problem. (Verse 30 is most unfortunate. Try explaining it to your congregation!) We should ask ourselves these questions:

   a. What am I doing here? If we find ourselves simply going through the motions, we should find some way of bringing ourselves up short, some way of catching our attention. Each time we approach the Communion table it would help to have something to remind us. Perhaps make a plan always to look at the cross up front or some such strategy to help get focused on why we are there.

   b. What should I think about? Just as in worship in general, there are many elements to the experience. We can concentrate on being thankful, or we can seek peace and composure. Probably two concerns to keep uppermost would be: 1) Our need to repent for our sins and seek the forgiveness that brings sincere change (as Paul reminds us in v. 28, "examine yourself"); and 2) Remembering what Jesus did on the cross (as v. 29 suggests, "recognize the meaning of Communion"). Jesus says, "Remember me" (vv. 24 and 25), when taking the bread and the cup.

   c. Will I leave a different person? Doing the previous two exercises in meditation will go a long ways toward making the answer to this question affirmative. But it would be efficacious to look ahead and ask, "How do I need to change?" Most of us are aware of the areas in our lives due for reconstruction. This is a time of new and renewed commitments.

D-10. Everything You Always Wanted To Know About The Bible Because You Were Afraid I'd Ask

Purpose Statement: *Occasionally there needs to be a sermon just on the general background of the Bible as a whole.*

When the preacher came to call, the woman of the house asked her daughter to go get the "big book Mommy reads out of all the time" (the last phrase intended to impress the preacher). The daughter returned with the Sears catalog. Knowing that far too many church members do not read, nor are they very familiar with the Bible, it behooves us every so often to preach on the general background of the scriptures to encourage more interest. One such sermon could be on four ways to know our Bibles.

a. Know the stories and details. We tend to know, in a general way, the popular stories of the Bible: Adam and Eve, Noah and the Ark, Daniel and the Lion's Den, and so forth. We know some details such as: Jesus was born in Bethlehem and died on the cross. For example, we believe we know how many wise men visited Jesus upon the occasion of his birth. But do we? Go back and read the account one more time to get the exact number. This kind of knowledge comes naturally from regular Bible use, but isn't very helpful in and of itself. We need more depth.

b. Know selected quotes. There is a tendency (especially among conservatives and fundamentalists) to memorize certain key verses that apply to specific concerns or issues such as: how we get saved, the place of women in the church, bits on the second coming, etc. This method is usually very selective. Passages are picked supporting a favored idea, and other related passages that may contradict the desired position are ignored. These memorized verses are kept ready to spring on some future debater. This knowledge remains narrowly focused.

c. Know the historical background. It is important to understand the setting for each verse, passage, or book in order to have a holistic or total picture and be assured of drawing the proper or intended meaning from it. This approach gives us more helpful knowledge with an over-all perspective.

d. Know it theologically. To be honest with scriptures, one has to consider everything the Bible has to say about any given issue, and then sort out differing views (i.e. The Old Testament has many passages recommending vengeance. The New Testament is strong on turning the other cheek, repudiating revenge). There are so many conflicting passages concerning salvation that need to be sorted out for a more comprehensive view. This approach is by far the most helpful.

E.

E-1. How To Handle Your Preacher

Purpose Statement: *Ministers could take the Sunday morning service as an opportunity to discuss the relationships between clergy and laity and the expectations each has of the other.*

It is a great opportunity to help the congregation understand the pastor, the task and pressures of the position, and how to relate to the pastor. Throughout my ministry I noticed so many instances where clergy and church members were less than enamored with each other. Communication may not solve all problems, but it is a significant beginning. (Remember the joke about the minister appointed to a church noted for the short stay of their pastors? After the minister had been there for an unprecedented six years, much longer than the previous fifteen pastors, he screwed up his courage and asked about it. The board chairperson told the pastor, "We really don't want a minister and you are the closest to not being one we ever had.") I can think of few scriptures that might speak directly to the subject. Philippians 2:19-30 might fill the gap. Possible suggestions to share with the congregation could include:

a. Use your minister. Never hesitate to communicate with her. A pastor never wants to hear that you didn't bring a concern to her because you "didn't want to bother her." Be up front and explain that a clergyperson must walk the fine line of seeming busy while not giving the impression of being too busy for you.

b. Serve with her. Clergy are not paid to do the layperson's religious work. In the Protestant tradition, the layperson is a co-pastor with the vicar and they serve in ministry together. The church is your family and the preacher is your sister or brother.

c. Be serious about getting to know and understand the pastor. Laypersons should never have expectations of the clergy they don't have for themselves. Proper conduct for clergy is appropriate conduct for everyone. Let the congregation know that pastors may sometimes be hurt and disappointed. Laypeople need to know when they miss a sermon on Sunday, they missed a masterpiece. Clergy must act as an unbiased third party sometimes in disputes. Church members must feel free to differ with, and still love, their pastor ... plus many more secrets.

E-2. How Many Roads To Heaven?

Purpose Statement: *Do we have to be a Christian or a certain kind of Christian to "get to heaven"?*

We've all heard someone (perhaps even ourselves) say, "We're all going to the same place; we're just taking different roads." A church member could legitimately ask the question, "Which is the true way?" Is it Christianity as opposed to other faiths, or a particular brand of Christianity? Or do all roads lead to heaven? Most of us end up with some form of religious belief, having probably arrived there by one of three ways.

   a. Raised Christian. Most people are what they are because they were born into a family that raised them with those beliefs. We don't often change, and when we do, it tends to be from one set of beliefs to another that is very similar. We are conditioned little by little as we grow up. It is sort of like a vaccination or inoculation — little doses at a time. This method leaves little dramatic impact and it is easy to drift into the complacency of a dry routine. We tend not to struggle with our doctrines and are not likely to work out our faith with fear and trembling. In a sense we gradually become a Christian as we mature.

   b. Converted to Christianity. They say converts are the most enthusiastic and loyal. The newly converted are usually charged up with excitement. It is on this avenue that we find the born-again experience. This doesn't mean the born-again experience doesn't happen to the person who is raised a Christian. Many mainline Christians would understand that being born again can and should happen over and over again because we believe that backsliding can happen.

c. Christian by comparison-shopping. Some arrive at their faith persuasion by looking at all of the options available, and after careful consideration, choose the best. As Christian pastors we believe that the teachings of Jesus stand head and shoulders above all other religious beliefs, both in terms of ethical and moral principles, and in the revelation of God's will.

This message must deal with passages such as: John 14:6, Matthew 7:13 14, and 21:28 31. Someone will say when you take a load of corn to the mill, the miller will not ask which road you took to get there. However, which road we choose does make a difference. It may be too roundabout and take too long, be rutted and dangerous causing you to lose some of the load, or confusing enough to get you lost.

E-3. Are There Any Goats In Heaven?

Purpose Statement: *Who is saved and how?*

To some extent what we think about heaven, who is going, and why, can determine how we act towards others or at least affect our attitudes concerning others. We don't know very much about "heaven," and unfortunately, the Bible bears conflicting witness on just how we get there. Paul emphasizes salvation by faith while Jesus, for every one statement implying salvation by faith, makes ten or more statements emphasizing works. The simple truth of this dilemma is that true faith and real works are inseparable (James 2:18, 24, 26).

Let us look at the beautiful parable of the sheep and goats (Matthew 25:31-46):

a. They seem to be saved by works. They fed the hungry and ministered to the sick. Faith and works are like the heart and mind of the body; we cannot survive without both. It would seem pointless to debate which is the most important.

b. They seem to be unaware they were saved. The most amazing part of this parable is that the sheep appear oblivious to their "saved" condition. The message seems to be "forget about getting saved; just love and serve people." Jesus said something about losing your life if you seek to save it and vice versa.

c. It is possible some (or all) of the goats made it. Jesus' mention of eternal hell is no doubt an oriental, dramatic emphasis to underline the importance of loving and caring for others. It would be unconscionably uncharacteristic of Jesus and God to hold out an eternity of burning punishment to threaten us to be good. I like the comment (Matthew 21:31) about the prostitutes and evil tax collectors getting to heaven ahead of the religious folk.

Are we really saved by a magic formula or pledge of allegiance, or by who and what we are (Matthew 21:28-31)? Heaven cannot be heaven unless my family is there no matter what they believe. And (as a conservative friend assured me), "If some of our loved ones don't make it, God will simply make us forget them," seems despicable.

E-4. When And How To Break The Law

Purpose Statement: *Are good Christian citizens ever allowed to break the civil law?*

Romans 13:1-7 tells us that civil law serves God's purpose and we should all respect it. In fact, we need the law to keep an orderly society. A Christian obeys the law, not for legalism's sake, but because the law exists to help others and us. The question is: Do we ever have permission to break the laws? I am going to say, "Yes." Then I would have to explain.

a. When? Since we do not live in a perfect world it stands to reason that some of our laws are inappropriate. One of our busiest tasks as humans is making and changing the law, with the object of getting it as close to right as possible. As Christians, we are called to obey two sets of laws: God's law and civil law. There are bound to be clashes between the two. When the two require two different postures of us, I am going to vote for deciding in favor of divine law. While Paul admonished us to obey our government and its laws, he, himself, disobeyed the authorities, choosing God's law instead. At the moment when Paul was writing this passage to the Romans, the issue of any discrepancy between divine and human law was not under discussion. If it had been, we can be assured Paul would have advised obeying God explicitly. Christians have disobeyed the law as conscientious objectors protesting wars, and violated immoral segregation laws to help usher in civil rights. God's law must never be broken.

b. How? 1) The first step is always to attempt to change immoral laws. Organize petitions, write or visit legislators, and participate in protest marches. Most Christians seldom if ever participate in these necessary activities. 2) If legal methods fail, it is time to be willing to bring the community's attention to the injustice through challenging the law. This has to be done peacefully, nonviolently, and with dignity, respect, and love.

c. Then what? Suffer the consequences! We must be prepared to pay the price, which could mean going to jail. This is another opportunity to witness. It sends the message that we are not vandals or anti-social deviants; but we are good citizens who care and only seek justice. When legislatures fail to respond, often an arrest will give the court system an opportunity to consider the issue.

70

E-5. Christianity Is Not A Majority Rules Activity

Purpose Statement: *Christianity is sensitive to all persons and no minorities should be overlooked or forgotten.*

Democracy is such a dominant and important concept in human affairs that it colors our impressions of Christianity. It is easy to assume that in all situations it will be "majority rules." That always seems fair and, if anything, Christianity plays fair. It is just that our faith goes beyond "what is allowed" or "what we may be legally responsible for." Jesus sent us the "second mile" and asked that we "turn the other cheek." He told parables such as the one where the eleventh hour workers were paid the same as the folks who worked all day (Matthew 20). If we are sued for one of our garments we should give the plaintiff another garment in good faith. Christianity seems to go beyond what is fair and safe. It calls for more. Luke 15 contains three parables that express this idea: the "prodigal son," the "lost coin," and the story concerning 99 sheep safe in the fold and the shepherd going out to find the one that is lost. Jesus said the well do not need a physician; the sick do.

    a. Minority needs. Christianity stresses serving the poor and unfortunate. It never intends for the majority to be ignored, or that all people aren't important and worthy of our concern. What Christianity simply says is the majority is often satisfied at the expense of the minority, and since the majority's needs are taken care of we must concentrate on the persons who have more serious needs. The 99 sheep are safe; go take care of the lost one.

    b. The minority is often right. In a democracy, the majority, right or wrong, will decide and rule. Christianity says that at times the majority may be wrong and the minority is right. In that case Christianity urges consideration of the minority's point of view however difficult that may be. Consequently, we have protest marches and civil rights demonstrations. At the very least the minority rights must be protected.

c. The minority has power. Finally, we need to appreciate the strength of the determined few! Analogous to the David and Goliath story, there is power in small numbers. Never underestimate what a few may do. A small boy with a few loaves and fishes can do wonders with Jesus' help.

E-6. How To Create A Frankenstein Monster

Purpose Statement: *How society treats certain persons often determines their personalities and dispositions. Christians must love all persons.*

We are commanded as Christians to love everyone and to treat all with the utmost kindness and respect. Society doesn't always do that however. We are well aware of the abuses some persons are subjected to. Christians must be sensitive to the feelings of those who are socially ostracized and love them. Jesus used a dinner invitation illustration to instruct us to care for the unfortunate or those whom society tends to overlook (Luke 14:12-14). Let me affirm the truth of three propositions:

a. Proposition #1: We have made personal appearance far too important. We revere the pretty people and honor them, as illustrated by Miss America contests. Sociological studies have shown how attractive people get the attention, jobs, and promotions and are generally enthusiastically received by society. By contrast persons deemed ugly or deformed or unpleasant to look at are shunned and rejected.

b. Proposition #2: Our reaction to a person's appearance can shape his or her personality. People are sensitive enough to the reaction of others to know when they are accepted or rejected. They are well aware they are either popular or disliked, or perhaps somewhere in between. This becomes a powerful influence on how they feel about themselves. We, in fact, have the power to shape the personalities of other people by our response to their appearance. Children sometimes pick on or humiliate classmates whose appearance is unattractive. This cruelty can be felt keenly. I remember a pathetic-looking little girl in about the second grade who no one would sit next to. There was one chair left and one student standing. The class chanted, "Ha, Ha, you have to sit next to ugly old Alice!"

c. Proposition #3: We can make other people into monsters or losers. Just as an abused dog can either turn mean or turn into a cowering wimp, persons can respond to rejection in different ways. Society can create a mean-spirited, bitter loner who takes a gun and kills others. Or society can cause a person to be depressed and even commit suicide. Christians have great opportunities to salvage lives. Who are you inviting to dinner?

E-7. No Chance For The Christian

Purpose Statement: *A Christian doesn't gamble.*

Ecclesiastes 5:10-14 warns us (as does Jesus many times) against an inordinate concern over money. Greed is alive and well and most of us struggle with the associated temptations. When we understand the principles upon which gambling is founded, we will understand why a Christian should refrain. Some will say, "Life is a gamble," or "Farming is a gamble." The following points will indicate how far gambling and life are from being analogous with each other. The first three points define gambling and the fourth point adds another reason for abstaining.

a. Gambling is getting something for nothing. This negates the work ethic: an honest day's wage for an honest day's work. One could hardly say farming is getting something for nothing. (Welfare is necessary when people are desperate, and only temporary, until they can get back on their feet or achieve employment.) Working is necessary for one's own self-respect. We all need to feel we are useful and are making a difference in our world.

b. Gambling is relying on chance or luck. One could hardly label a farmer's plowing, planting, cultivating, fertilizing, and irrigating as relying on luck. Only a fool doesn't dream, plan, organize, and build to achieve the goal. We provide for health care coverage and plan for retirement; we don't trust to chance.

c. Gambling is taking from others and giving nothing in return. Gambling is taking from the many to give to the one. Farming in contrast is the one giving to the many. Gambling is getting as much from others as we can without regard for them. Christianity, in contrast, is giving to others in need.

d. Gambling is hopelessly connected with anti-social consequences: crime, sickness (addiction), and family destruction. Reno and Las Vegas have inordinately high crime rates, suicide above the national average, murder rates higher than much larger cities, and abnormal welfare.

It is sad when communities and governments must rely on lotteries and other forms of gambling to raise money. Appeal to greed will do what an appeal to conscience or patriotism won't.

E-8. Zacchaeus, The Widow, And Jacob's Deal

Purpose Statement: *A sermon on knowing how much to give God.*

It is not uncommon for stewardship sermons to be unwelcome with both preacher and listeners. Finding new ideas and ways to speak about this important subject is difficult. I suggest the interesting juxtaposition of three biblical incidents.

a. Jacob's deal. Genesis 28:18-23 tells the amusing story of Jacob making a deal with God at Bethel. He is about to set off on a journey and if God will protect him and make his trip successful, he promises to give God one tenth of the profits. I'm sure this pleased God.

b. Zacchaeus' better deal. Luke 19:1-8 relates how, after meeting Jesus at Jericho, Zacchaeus claims he will give half of his possessions to the poor. He had a much bigger vision than Jacob. And if he had cheated anyone he would repay that person back four times the amount. Jacob was thinking of self, Zacchaeus of others.

c. The widow tops them all. Luke 21:1-4 has Jesus raising the stakes. Watching a poor widow put all she had, with no strings attached, in the Temple's treasury, he applauds her act. I still feel that Jesus used exaggeration to make dramatic emphasis on many occasions: i.e. the camel through a needle's eye, etc. (and often these are related to wealth and attitudes towards wealth). He would not actually want the poor woman to give everything away. He was, instead, shaming those who had wealth and telling us we are not giving enough.

I have always preached (and if you disagree, move on to the next sermon) that the proper amount to give to church is not necessarily a tithe of ten percent. It may be the appropriate sum for some folks, but there are situations that call for less and more. Ten percent for the poor is excessive. Giving is rewarding and the ability to give is good for our self-esteem. However, giving away money needed to feed the baby is foolish even if you think God will provide. There are millions of starving children testifying that God doesn't always step in and rescue. At the other end of the spectrum, there are very many people whose incomes warrant a high percentage of charitable giving indeed. Those with ridiculously high-level incomes need to think in terms of the eighty or ninety percent range. It all starts with appreciation for life and sincere concern for others.

E-9. Jonah And The Fish That Got Away

Purpose Statement: *The intent is to show the great love and forgiveness of God and our own humanness in the difficult struggle to emulate that love.*

Jonah may be my favorite story in the Old Testament. Not the first part that is so well-known. But the second half of the story after Jonah failed to catch his fish. Most people can't remember "the rest of the story" (as Paul Harvey would say) because the first part is so graphic. The first two chapters tell about the fish that got away. The second two chapters tell another fascinating story of Jonah letting a second fish get away. He missed his opportunity to celebrate a forgiveness and compassion for a city he successfully saved. At least he was honest about his human shortcomings. Three very interesting things emerge.

a. Jonah was a success. He was asked to go preach to Nineveh, a great and apparently wicked city. His message was to be that God would destroy the entire city because they were so sinful. The city only had forty days. They fasted and repented. God saw how they changed from their wicked ways; Jonah had converted the whole city. (All this in chapter 3.)

b. But Jonah wanted to fail. The rest of this interesting story concludes in chapter 4. He became angry over the salvation of Nineveh and honestly admitted to God that God's forgiveness of the city greatly disappointed him. From Jonah's very human perspective, the city deserved severe punishment and should perish.

c. The final episode finds Jonah more concerned over a dead plant than over all the people of the great city. A big catch got away as forgiveness and compassion alluded Jonah's sympathies. Perhaps we get more riled up over a smashed fender on our car or getting home with a new purchase only to find it was defectively made, than we do over the fact that countless children are starving in Ethiopia or Afghanistan.

The moral of the story: we need a greater concern for our practice of God's love and forgiveness.

E-10. Better Moonshine!

Purpose Statement: *Since "prohibition didn't work" is often used as an argument for not making other troubling activities illegal, all of us need to become aware that prohibition did work and the conditions during prohibition were much better than before or after.*

It is better to have moonshine, bathtub gin, or illegal alcohol than to have legalized drink ravaging our society. What hardly anyone knows today due to the propaganda of the liquor industry and the unwitting cooperation of the news media is that prohibition worked!

   a. Begin with a recitation of the tremendous cost of drinking in destruction of lives and family life. We dread cancer and yet we invite health problems and even death into our lives by using alcohol. Studies show around seventy percent of crime and about fifty percent of highway deaths are related to drinking. (Proverbs 23:29-35 is descriptive.)

   b. Tell the true story of prohibition. While we have been brainwashed to believe otherwise, literature exists that reveals the truth that conditions under prohibition were far better than before or after, though it is hard to come by. One of the best sources is the book *Drinking in America: A History*, published in 1987 by The Free Press. Interestingly enough, it is not anti-drinking. If anything, it is pro-drinking. And yet pages 136-139 are a powerful testimony concerning the truth about how successful prohibition really was.

   c. State why Christians shouldn't drink.

   1. It destroys your health.

   2. It impairs your ability to be rational.

   3. You are an influence on others. (1 Corinthians 8:9-13, Romans 14:13-21)

   4. By drinking you keep a destructive industry alive.

   5. Drinking supports using 10,000 tons of grain a day for destruction while 10,000 people starve.

   6. Drinking serves no good purpose whatsoever.

77

F.

F-1. Why Is Christianity Polarized?

Purpose Statement: *Christianity's many denominations and sects seem to fall into two very general camps. Since Christians need to build unity and cooperation, understanding our differences is necessary.*

The term usually denoting a more liberal Christian is "mainline" while a more conservative Christian is identified as "evangelical." In many communities the ministers from these two perspectives cannot get along and seldom cooperate on anything, and will usually even have two separate ministerial fellowships. (See sermon D-4 for related discussion.) These divisions have plagued our church from the beginning (1 Corinthians 1:10-13) and the need to make one undivided witness to the world is important (Ephesians 4:1-6).

The general reason for our polarization is the way we choose to understand and interpret our Bible.

a. The "conservative" tends to claim the Bible is perfect with no contradictions while the "liberal" understands the Bible to be written by humans with human errors. Examples of the many apparent contradictions would be: Judas's death in Matthew 27 and Acts 1; Saul's death in 1 Samuel 31 and 2 Samuel 1; the one or two donkey problem in Matthew 21:1-3 and Mark 11:1-3 (also Luke 19 and John 12); or the Nazareth or Bethlehem problem in Matthew 2:22-23 and Luke 2:39. The only way to rationalize the differences is to "read into" scripture what isn't there or to manipulate words which the conservative must do to be satisfied! Or admit some contradictions.

b. Consequently, the conservative wants a literal, and the liberal, sometimes, a figurative approach to interpretation.

c. Both are prone to very selective choices of passages for enlightenment and will avoid other "inconvenient" passages.

78

d. Neither side will listen to the other point of view for fear their faith will be jeopardized. But that is exactly what needs to happen. We must encourage dialogue. Perhaps before that will happen, better relationships can be established in small group cooperation on projects of a neutral nature.

F-2. Living Courteously On A Crowded Planet

Purpose Statement: *A very good sermon needs to be preached every so often concerning being a good neighbor and being thoughtful to others.*

Romans 14:13-23 is an excellent passage about monitoring our behavior in order to be a good neighbor or to help other people. The passage concerns not eating food dedicated to idols if it would lead someone else into trouble. I think we all could agree that this passage can honestly be extrapolated to mean other behavior than only eating food.

a. The crowd. Our planet is becoming more crowded and more of us are living much closer to many more neighbors than ever before. Experiments with mice reveal they are prone to anti-social behavior and psychological problems when subjected to over-crowded conditions. We need "our space" and quiet time. Some folks are lucky to live in sparsely-settled areas. But too many live up close to their neighbors and spend an hour driving to and from work each day in bumper-to-bumper frustration.

b. The condition. The results include: road rage, employees shooting their co-workers, kids taking guns to school to shoot their peers, tavern brawls, stress sending people home to abuse their family, and the list goes on. A great deal of our activity will affect other persons. We don't want to be bothered. But are we irritating others by our activity? "My freedom ends where another person's nose begins" is too true.

c. The control. We need to be reminded of the many ways we can be a good neighbor and not irritate others. Don't use your loud lawn mower when you know a neighbor is resting. Don't play your music so loudly. Don't litter. Don't straddle the lines to take up two parking spaces. Keep pets in your own yard and quiet. Don't trample others at rock concerts or soccer matches. Be courteous in traffic. Don't leave your shopping carts strewn over the parking lot. Walk instead of drive when possible. Don't always look for a parking spot in the lot closest to the door (you need the walk! and the closer spot might help an elderly person). And a legion more. In other words, we can stop being slobs. Jesus said something about doing unto other people, as we would want them to do for us.

F-3. Hoping God Won't Answer — Until...!

Purpose Statement: *We need to confess that sometimes we are so audacious as to want a relationship with God on our terms!*

So many of the Psalms are cries for help and some of them express the idea that God has let us down or isn't there to help us. Many believe that Jesus might have quoted the entire 22nd Psalm from the cross, and not just the first line only, which asks why God had forsaken him. It would make sense if he did quote the entire psalm. Psalm 13 is another example of one desperately seeking God. This leads to some important thoughts.
a. When we don't want God there! Let us confess there are times when acknowledging the presence of God would be uncomfortable. This is true especially when we are doing wrong. We also avoid God when we think that an honest encounter at that moment would require some change or sacrifice we are unwilling to endure. How often do we believe that we can go it alone without God?
b. When we do want God there! In other words, it may be convenient to ignore God until a problem arises we can't

solve or a disaster strikes. Then we want help and expect it now! Disaster brings people out of the woodwork and into church. History has given us sufficient examples where tragedy sends people looking for God. The destruction of the World Trade Center Towers is such an incident. God probably wants to ask some of us, "Where were you last week?" Secretly, we hope God won't bother us until we need God.

c. When God may not be there! Like many other passages in the Psalms, the first line of Psalm 13 gives the impression that God isn't there. "God, how much longer before you help me? Will you forget me forever?" (This is a paraphrase.) The reason why God is hard to find during trial is that we didn't establish a previous working relationship. You may not be much of a piano player if you never learned to play. And even if you learned, you may not do well if you haven't practiced for a long time. If we do not save a little money in the bank, there won't be anything there in time of need. Don't wait for tragedy to have a faith relationship with God.

d. When God comes back. (Some people say if God isn't near, it wasn't God who moved!) Psalm 13 follows the pattern of many psalms, by asking for help, being disappointed if it is not forthcoming, and finally testifying to a great faith in God anyway! This psalm ends with confidence that God will finally help and so God is praised. The solution is persistence in our search for God. Remember Jesus' promise if we ask, seek, and knock.

F-4. Columns Of Stone Or Coals Of Fire?

Purpose Statement: *Revenge has no place in the Christian's repertoire.*

With the bombing of the World Trade Center September 11, 2001 (as I write this, smoke is still coming from the ruins a few

81

days later), there was an outcry for revenge. We must kill them. Even the president demeaned himself with violent rhetoric claiming we would go to war, a war the likes of which has never been seen before. The show of hate was depressing. However, the outpouring of letters and comments asking for peace, restraint, and no retaliation shocked me! There was a greater showing of common sense than I would have expected. I think society is seeing some growth towards real civilization, perhaps. In a continuum of virtues, love is at the top and hate at the bottom. Yet society still expresses so much hate and desire for revenge. Every Christian is required to abstain absolutely from feelings of hate, violence, and revenge. Jesus' teachings (Matthew 5:38-48, one of many examples) and Paul's reiteration (Romans 12:9-21) leave no doubt as to what our posture should be regarding the proper response to insult, hate, and violence. Two contrasting scriptures illustrate the extremes. From the Old Testament (where one can unfortunately find many violent passages) comes the story of Samson's revenge (Judges 16:23-30). After being blinded by the Philistines he is able to grab the columns of the building where people were gathered and pull down the columns, bringing the building crashing down on his enemies. Compare this with the Christian teaching of Paul in the Romans 12 selection cited above where our love will bring coals of fire upon our enemies' heads. It doesn't mean hurt or harm. The *Good News Bible* uses the phrase "burn with shame." Reasons why vengeance is wrong would include:

a. Revenge brings revenge in return. It is a vicious circle. The same hate that produced the revenge will be exacerbated into more hate by the revenge. World War II grew out of the bitter feelings left over from World War I. The World Trade Center incident was partially spawned by the Persian Gulf altercation among others.

b. Revenge eliminates our chance for healing and reconciliation. Someone has to stop the escalation and show maturity and be civilized. If either Israel or the Palestinians — just one — would stop the terrorism against the other, peace could be worked out. Which group will be adult enough to stop "getting even"?

c. Revenge destroys the revenger! Hate eats us up. In some cases it can do more harm than the original insult. Then the enemy has two victories over us!

F-5. The Famous Anonymouses Of The Bible

Purpose Statement: *A sermon intent on keeping us humble, as well as keeping our motives more altruistic in our service to others.*

Jesus urged us to not let our one hand know what the other hand was doing. Remember, exaggeration was his way of making his point emphatic. Do alms in secret so no one will know (Matthew 6:2-4).

a. There is a list of significant unknowns. A few of the famous anonymouses of the Bible would include (any of which could become the main scripture) the widow who dropped all she had into the offering (Luke 21:1-4), the woman who anointed Jesus at Bethany and who would be "remembered all over the world" (Matthew 26:6-13), the Roman officer of "great faith" (Matthew 8:5-10), the good Samaritan (Luke 10:23-37), the boy who offered his five loaves and two fish to feed 5,000 (John 6:1-13), the criminal on the cross who was saved (Luke 23:39-43), the soldier at the cross who claimed Jesus was the Son of God (Matthew 27:54), and the wise men and shepherds at his birth.

b. Add your "name" to the list. Again, Jesus is overdramatizing the anonymity. He would and did suggest that we witness and let our light shine. However, his point is to keep our motives pure. We shouldn't be doing good for our own glorification. It isn't easy to do good in secret and not get credit. I once shoveled the snow from the parsonage walks, and then the next-door neighbor's walk, and then the church walks next to her. When I returned home from the church she came out and said, "Wasn't that nice of the fraternity men across the street to shovel our walks?" I set her straight.

Humility is a part of the Christian lifestyle and so is doing well solely for the sake of others.

c.   And get on God's list. The idea that God will reward you (Matthew 6:4) would seem to negate the effort to avoid self-promotion. However, the reward is not praise, heaven, riches, or other obvious honors. The reward is satisfaction and personal self-fulfillment. It is knowing you are growing. It is the peace and joy that comes with Christian serving.

F-6. What Made Jesus Cry?

Purpose Statement: *A sermon encouraging us to be more sensitive to others.*

Two instances where Jesus wept are recorded in our Bible. John 11:28-35 records the death of Lazarus. It is indicated that Jesus cried both over his death and because of the sorrow of the family. A second occasion for his tears is reported in Luke 19:41-44 when he weeps over the people of Jerusalem because they have not found peace and joy in life. Their ignorance as to how to make peace will cause them to suffer at an enemy's hands. (A case could be made for a third occasion in Gethsemane.) Weeping is not a sign of weakness! Depending on the reason, it can be an indication of love and compassion. We would expect Jesus to be hurt because of the hurt of others. It is important for us to deal with our own compassion! Among many possibilities, here are three significant relationships:

a.   Sensitivity to the suffering of others and understanding! I really believe that such sensitivity is evidence that people are thoughtful, alert to the problems and hurts of others. It doesn't mean they are smarter. However, they enjoy a wisdom and maturity of understanding not given to others, including others who may be more "intelligent." Such sensitive people think about (while others tend to ignore) others who are involved in car accidents, war, poverty, health issues, starvation, deep depression, abused children, suffering animals, and the list goes on! They pause in sadness for a moment of prayer! They don't forget! They don't say, "I'll just put that out of my mind."

b. Sensitivity to the suffering of others and appreciation of beauty! Those who can feel more keenly the hurt of other persons must also have a heightened total sensitive nature, I suspect. This would mean they are more alive to everything around them. They experience beauty and have joy in great music, flowers, clouds, animals, and the grandeur of the universe! They walk through life more open and receptive, without blinders.

c. Sensitivity to the suffering of others and love! It seems natural these two virtues are intricately linked. True empathy and sympathy will increase love, while our love will make us care about the condition of all others. In each of these three suggestions, every person has a potential to develop this sensitivity that brings fullness of life!

What makes you cry?

F-7. Advice Your Attorney Won't Give You

Purpose Statement: *A much-ignored mandate given by Jesus, "going the second mile," needs serious consideration.*

There are several teachings of Jesus that we find very difficult to accept or practice. Jesus said that if someone sues you for your shirt, give that person your coat as well (Matthew 5:40). Who does that? Your attorney would never give you that advice, nor would anyone else for that matter. People would consider you crazy to follow such a suggestion. Yet history has extensive examples of this kind of love, the chief example being Jesus going to the cross and forgiving those who killed him. We have all heard of beautiful stories similar to the incident where a couple adopted the seventeen-year-old boy who, while driving drunk, killed their only son.

Call them fools, but until the world has more people like them, we will continue to have too much hate in the world.

   a. Three philosophies are reflected in the Good Samaritan story (Luke 10:25-37).
      1. The thief says, "What is yours is mine and I'll take it!"
      2. The priest and Levite say, "What is mine is mine and I'll keep it!"
      3. The Samaritan says, "What is mine is yours and I'll share it!"
   b. Many find ways of objecting to uncomfortable teachings of Jesus.
      1. Jesus didn't intend it, at least for us.
      2. It won't work.
      3. When the other person does it first, then I'll turn the other cheek.

We still have the Golden Rule: "Do unto others as you want them to do to you," which is found in some form in the sacred writings of other religions.

F-8. How Many Will Your Garbage Can Feed?

Purpose Statement: *Pastors must repeat sermons on our need to stop wasting food and overeating, coupled with more giving to the world's starving.*

   Jesus urged us to be compassionate and to feed the hungry. Along with the classic final judgment parable (Matthew 25:31-46), one could add his mandate to Peter to feed his sheep (John 21:15-17), the rich man and the poor man (Luke 16:19-31), and others. We get tired of hearing about this subject. We can imagine some suffering children in the world who are tired of starving also! I repeat what I have said before: a Christian cannot afford to grow weary of hearing about the needs of others. Paul said (Galatians 6:9) we cannot get tired of doing good.
   a. Use the startling figures on the world's starving as well as some dramatic instances to keep a graphic picture before

the congregation. There are a lot of facts available such as: fifteen to thirty million die of hunger each year; one billion are undernourished; 75 percent of these people are children. One absolutely amazing fact we are told is hunger causes overpopulation instead of diminishing population!

b. Have the congregation honestly consider the amount of food each of us throws away and how much harmful over-eating we do. Each of our garbage cans could literally feed other people. They do! Some people in our cities are getting their food out of dumpsters! I know I should not have as much to eat as I do as long as others are hungry!

c. Make the situation more real and personal by imagining that the starving child is our daughter or son or grandchild. Would we turn away a starving child literally knocking on our door? They *are* knocking on our door!

F-9. Out Of Sight; Out Of Mind: The Ostrich Approach To World Hunger

Purpose Statement: *Inwardly we groan when we hear another sermon on starving people in our world. Consequently we need a sermon on our reaction to such sermons!*

We preach a lot about it and so did Jesus. Mass hunger has always been with us and we hear constantly about it. We get tired of hearing about it and that is something a Christian can never afford to do — get tired of hearing about human need! Jesus went through the little ritual with Peter (John 21:15-19) three times urging him to feed his sheep. We have the story of the rich man who ignored the starving man at his gate (Luke 16:19-31). Amos 4:1-3 echoes the concern. We read where John Wesley, when he was 84, went begging for four days in winter to collect money for food to feed the poor.

a. The problem is great! Start this kind of sermon with some of the startling figures concerning the numbers of people starving in the world today, and compare the cost of feeding a specific number with the money we spend on alcohol, smoking, movies, desserts, bowling, video games, skiing, feeding and grooming our pets, or creating armaments for war.

b. We are frustrated with it! 1) The constant reminders about world hunger irritate us or make us uncomfortable. 2) The problem seems too vast and what we can do as one person seems so small in contrast. 3) We are afraid of what kind of sacrifices it may require on our part if we take an interest and get serious about the problem.

c. Often our solution is to forget! We deal with many problems with this gimmick. Just put it out of our mind. Don't think about it. If we isolate or insulate ourselves from the facts and faces of hunger, the frustration seems to go away.

d. The counter-solution is to be reminded. We need pesky preachers to keep before us the stark reality that so many people are starving. Please don't shoot the messenger!

Remember this little rhyme? "There upon the stair / I saw a man who wasn't there / He wasn't there again today / Oh, how I wish he'd go away."

F-10. What Are You Doing Out Of Jail?

Purpose Statement: *As Christians we should be social activists using nonviolent protests to bring justice and peace to our communities and world.*

It is reported that a friend visiting Henry David Thoreau in jail asked him why he was there, and Thoreau answered with a question also, "What are you doing out of jail?"

a. The really great leaders usually have been in jail. Most of the biblical prophets and religious leaders, including Jesus, have been hunted down, arrested, jailed, or killed. (This does not include the establishment religious leaders such as the Pharisees.) Acts 4 tells the story of Peter and John, and perhaps other disciples, being thrown in jail for saying things that offended the Jewish leaders. When they were released, they were admonished not to continue — but they did. In one of the Beatitudes, Matthew 5:10-12, Jesus tells us we are blessed if we are persecuted for Christian work. Jesus predicts his followers would suffer arrest (Matthew 10:16-23), and there seems to be no reason why it couldn't apply to us today. Throughout history, great leaders like Ghandi and Martin Luther King have gone to jail because they sought to make our society more peaceful and just.

b. Why aren't you and I in jail? Has our world changed so much for the better that our protest and social activist work is no longer needed? Probably not! The point is the Christian should be concerned about the wrongs and injustices in our communities and doing something about it. We should be writing letters, picketing, joining groups committed to social change (MADD, NAACP, WCTU, Amnesty International, among many others), attending rallies, organizing, etc. Such activity brought great progress in the Civil Rights Movement. Racism, capital punishment, war, and many other social diseases continue. We should be busy.

c. One big obstacle is we cannot agree. Denial, apathy, and a host of other reasons prevent us from action. But one roadblock is the fact that we cannot agree on which position is right and wrong concerning many issues. Gun control, abortion, capital punishment are subjects that divide us. It is critical that the church assiduously study these problems until we reach a significant consensus! The Quakers, I am told, have a theory that when persons who really care sit down and prayerfully discuss and listen openly, they gradually gravitate towards the truth! I believe it. Why don't we try it?

G.

G-1. You Told Who?

Purpose Statement: *Mainline Christians need to get over their shyness and reluctance to witnessing.*

We are very uncomfortable with the kind of evangelism that some ardent Christians impose upon us (see C-3 and D-2). Consequently, and for other reasons also, mainline Christians do little or no evangelism. I think that it was Billy Graham who asked, "When did you last lead someone to Christ? When did you last try?" Even the way those questions are phrased makes some persons uncomfortable. That style of question may lead to a style of witness that scares more people than it wins. Jesus' sending out the twelve disciples (Luke 9:1-6) and 72 more of his followers (Luke 10:1-12) sends us the inescapable message that evangelism is our concern! Some humor making the rounds poses the question, "What do you get when you cross a Jehovah's Witness with a Unitarian? Someone who knocks on your door for no apparent reason."

    a. Tell others. Some faith communities do not believe in evangelism. It is not proper to "impose" one's religion on others, they say. Besides running contrary to the teachings of Jesus, that idea also does not make good sense. Anyone who has found something significant that others need should want to tell about it. Remember how the shepherds were excited over their experience with Jesus (Luke 2:20)? Do we lack that excitement? If you found a cure for cancer, you would be excited to share it with the world. In Jesus we have found something greater than the cure for cancer. We can't wait to spread gossip. We need that same enthusiasm for our church. We need to invite those without a faith connection to our church, instead of those who already have a religious home. Christians have been guilty of proselytizing too often. The major part of growth for some new churches comes from other churches instead of from unchurched persons.

b. Be the church. The best kind of evangelism is loving and serving in such a way that persons will be drawn into friendships or will be urged to inquire about your church. The concern should not be to "get people into church," but to serve the needs of people in the name of Christ. In our communities we must be serving, and in our church providing a healing, caring, nurturing, and supporting fellowship base that attracts others. Mainline church leaders are worried about losing members and begin to play the numbers game. If the church is dealing with real live issues that hurt people, it may even drive away those whose commitment is superficial, although the intent is never to drive anyone away. The intent is to be the church! Even Jesus wasn't always successful in winning followers (Luke 9:51-62, Matthew 13:53-58 and 19:16-22).

G-2. When God Hates To Go To Church!

Purpose Statement: *We should examine what worship is meant to be and how closely our worship approaches what God intends for us.*

Several times in scripture we are given some suggestions concerning what constitutes true worship. Sometimes this takes the form of severe criticism of the existing practice, the most dramatic of which is probably the time Jesus drove the assistant ministers and acolytes out of the church because they had made it a "den of thieves." More than one prophet made it very emphatic that it is not only unsightly, but also just plain wrong to burn animals on our altars as a form of worship. At least two of the prophets spoke very graphically. Isaiah 1:10-20 (use *Good News Bible: Today's English Version*) has God saying in reference to the people's worship, "I'm tired of ... It's useless ... I am disgusted ... I cannot stand ... I hate ... I will not look ... I will not listen...." Amos 5:21-24 uses the same strong language, "I hate your religious festivals."

There seem to be many possibilities of ways to attack this concern. You can certainly think of many.

a. When worship isn't real, we become hypocrites.
b. When worship isn't real, we gain nothing beneficial from it.
c. When worship isn't real, it will be reflected in our life. We will be more greedy, unjust, bitter, etc.

Or: Worship must be (a) freeing, (b) uplifting, (c) humbling, (d) unifying, etc.

Or endless other possibilities.

We can close with the question, "Does God hate to go to church with us?"

G-3. Beauty Is NOT In The Eye Of The Beholder!

Purpose Statement: *Our obsession with appearance causes us to discriminate.*

Jesus' teaching about possessions is also a warning against vanity (Matthew 6:28-33). If anything, we are overly concerned with how we look. It is the spiritual side of us (v. 33) that is important. Our souls or minds or personalities constitute the real "us" and our real value.

a. We revere physical beauty. We dote on the pretty people. We name them Miss America and Miss Universe. Consequently, our beauty contests say to the rest of us, "This is the ideal, what you are supposed to look like." The rest of us don't measure up. (I'm not knocking, "Black is beautiful," a very important concept that doesn't really have anything to do with outward appearance. It is a statement of the dignity and beauty all of us have.) We waste enormous amounts of money on cosmetics to look beautiful. In the process we also denigrate old age. Staying young is beautiful. Aging is abhorrent. Attractive people get the jobs, the promotions, and the attention.

b. Consequently, we miss the real beauty. The old adage that beauty is in the eye of the beholder, of course, means that each of us has different tastes. The physical appearance that attracts one person may not appeal to another. However, it is still an emphasis on the outward and superficial appearance. We know better: all persons are worthy, have dignity, and must have our respect. We just don't practice it. We are so conditioned from early childhood to judge persons by their physical appearance, and then to treat them or relate to them accordingly. It takes a concerted effort to overcome the habit. We must be very intentional about seeing all persons as equal in worth. We must value all differences as unique and beautiful. We must begin to treat all persons equally. To the extent that we do not, we are failing to see them as God's children and God's creation. We then denigrate God.

G-4. Born Again, And Again, And Again

Purpose Statement: *Christians need a comprehensive understanding about what it means to be born again.*

There are differences in opinion among Christians concerning what "being born again" entails. We should make efforts to clarify these misunderstandings. Eliminating the different ways people will interpret that concept is not possible. However, we should help persons appreciate why those different beliefs are held.

a. There is not one pattern of being born again! A perusal of conversion experiences of religious leaders would suffice to reveal the differences in each event. Moses, Isaiah, Peter, Andrew, Paul, Martin Luther, John Wesley, and the thief on the cross present a variety of initial religious experiences. Jesus explained to Nicodemus (John 3:1-8) about being transformed by God's Holy Spirit. (The mention of the "water" could, like the "great commission" at the end of Matthew, be considered an addition of the early church.

Surely, God does not condemn someone who has not been baptized. We wouldn't. Why believe in such a heartless God?) Jesus speaks of the ambiguity of the experience with the analogy of the wind blowing we know not where. It is mysterious and we do not understand it, but it happens. It could be sudden and it could be gradual. And it can happen in many ways. Not many of us have had fire drop down on our heads as we picture it did at Pentecost.

b. There is backsliding. Frankly, the notion that once you are saved, you can never sin again is preposterous. Don't you wish. How can anyone with a straight face make such a claim? Of course we continue to sin. It is unfortunate that some persons aren't recognizing their sins. The rest of us see their sins just as we recognize our need for repentance and forgiveness daily.

c. Being born again is a continuing process. Even when the born again experience is sudden and dramatic, it still remains a continuing process after that. How many self-righteous Christians have we seen who, after a conversion, now know everything and are perfect in their own opinion? Being a Christian means to choose to be reborn regularly or every day. It is a growing process of worship, prayer, and discipline.

A woman — a real saint — asked on her deathbed with serious apprehension, "Am I reborn?" She should have never needed to ask that question at that point in her life, a life that had been of impeccable Christian witness and service. She was led to her fears and doubts by a certain kind of preaching that unequivocally stated she must be reborn — their way!

G-5. Stop Putting Out God's Fires

Purpose Statement: *God is calling us and we aren't always listening or willing to respond.*

Exodus 3:1-15 tells the story of God calling Moses. The important question is: "Is God calling us?" How do we know and do we really want to know?

a. Want to know God's call? This is the critical test: if we are honest with ourselves, we may not want a call from God. It would require change, discipline, and perhaps sacrifice. We may not be ready and willing to commit ourselves. Moses put himself in the desert (v. 1) in a lonely occupation where he could think. We know the situation he left in Egypt would give him good reason for reflection.

b. Be observant. Burning bushes (vv. 2-3) will not always be that obvious. We must be alert to the possible kinds of calls. It can come through a feeling, or God may lead us through a rational process of thinking it out. It may come through another person's sharing with us. Some incident or emergency could be the occasion for God's needing you. Other people's needs may be your call.

c. Prepare for and expect God's presence. God told Moses to remove his shoes; he was on holy ground (v. 5). All ground is holy ground when we understand it. Taking off our shoes is a euphemism for us to be in prayer and meditation. Experiencing God's presence is the essence of worship where God will speak to us.

d. Be responsive. The excuses of Moses are legendary (v. 11). After God discounts one excuse, Moses comes up with another immediately. This chain of give-and-take is *apropos* to our own reluctance.

e. Be God's call for others. God's call to Moses was a call for others. God heard the cry of the people in Egypt (vv. 7 and 9) and wanted Moses to bring the burning bush to them. How many opportunities to share God's call have we ignored or refused?

G-6. You Can't Do That In Church!

Purpose Statement: *Getting out of ruts and old habits that have lost their purpose or meaning is difficult but necessary.*

It is a common and often-repeated complaint that some churches are so entrenched in the "way we have always done it" that new life is squelched.

a. You can't do things differently. I remember how our church became incensed over the introduction of *The Revised Standard Version* in the 1940s. It was distorting the truth of the Bible. I once argued with the church about changing the altar cloths to reflect the season colors of the church year instead of the plan they had. Perhaps I was the one unable to change and grow. Custodians, due to their care of the church, get into a routine, even to a point of possessiveness, and fight changes in property use. Some churches cannot take Communion but one way. Resistance can be severe to learning new hymns. "We like the old favorites." We've all seen it happen: after learning some of the very beautiful and theologically impressive new hymns, they soon become the "favorites."

b. You can't believe things differently. Jesus changed our beliefs. He quoted the Old Testament several times (Matthew 5) and then proceeded to tell us something different. We have changed our beliefs concerning animal sacrifice, polygamy, and eating pork, to mention just a few, but yet sternly resist growing theologically in many ways. We will cling to the notion the Bible is perfect with no contradictions. Just yesterday I read a letter to the newspaper stating that God brought about the airplane attack on the World Trade Center to teach us a lesson, even though it cost thousands of lives. When we cling to such outrageous beliefs, we have some growing to do.

c. You can't be different. We must allow each other to become new creations even when it frightens us.

G-7. How Big Is Your Family?

Purpose Statement: *Christians must fight racism in our communities and in ourselves.*

Two interesting incidents in the life of Jesus prompt us to enlarge our vision of what constitutes a family. In John 19:25-27 from the cross Jesus tells his mother and John they must regard themselves as mother and son from henceforth. In Matthew 12:46-50, Jesus, upon hearing that his family had arrived and were inquiring after him, told the crowd that whoever did God's will was his family. Jesus had a different concept of family, and if you asked him, he would tell you that every person is a child of God and your sister or brother. We don't share that vision. We exclude others, not only from our families, but also from our association. Racism is still one of our serious social problems.

   a. Examples. Discrimination in housing, employment, restaurants, and other sectors of our communities is well documented. Black students will be applauded by a teacher for a *C* while white students are given much higher expectations. As a pastor to a black church for fifteen years, I have personally witnessed racism and had church members tell me of many of their experiences. A church leader beyond the local church once asked me if our church didn't have "a black boy" on the police force, referring to one of our members in his upper forties. One of our members, a schoolteacher, was told by her aid that she couldn't work with her because she was black. One white teacher commented, "That kid smells because he is black." When our church visited another church for a service, one of our members was told not to use the bathroom. Being stopped regularly by the police for no other reason than being profiled is a regular occurrence.

   b. Results. One church member asked me one day, "What sin did we commit that caused God to make us black?" Racism had made him feel that being black was degrading and a punishment. Racism hurts people of color and white

97

people (in our communities whites are responsible for the preponderance of racism and institutional racism). Some crime by young African-Americans can be attributed to anger and hopelessness sparked by racism.

c. Causes. Racism is often the result of the low self-esteem of the racist. We do not feel as good about ourselves as we should and look around for others we can place in an inferior position. Skin color becomes an easy identification. Fear and ignorance are also important factors.

d. Cures. 1) We must stop the denial, admit our racist attitudes, and sincerely want to do something about it. 2) We can begin to read more to educate ourselves on the issue. 3) We should immerse ourselves in other cultures as much as possible when we have the opportunities.

How big is your family?

G-8. Getting Out Of Your Grave

Purpose Statement: *The resurrection message is of course the heart of the Christian faith and not just for Easter or funerals. This sermon is concerned with the reasons for eternal life. (J-10 is about evidence for eternal life and K-9 is about what eternal life might be like.)*

A woman took a shortcut through the cemetery going home from the late shift at work each night. One night, she fell into a newly dug grave along her path that she couldn't see in the dark. She was short and unable to get out, and finally sat in the corner to wait for day and help. Along came a man who fell in. The woman, sitting in the corner unobserved, watched to see if the man could get out and then she would call to him for help. He tried, but was unsuccessful. She finally spoke up and said, "I don't think you'll make it." But he did!

Everyone must die, probably fears death a little, and certainly wonders a lot about what lies beyond death. Many Christians maintain a faith that includes doubts. We believe in heaven, but we also

98

wonder. We do all we can to avoid death unless conditions in this life get too much for us. Any of the resurrection stories in scripture would be appropriate.

    a. Brings meaning to life. Everything takes its meaning from our lives. Without the human mind or soul to make sense of it, 3 x 3 = 9 means nothing. Great music and the beauty of nature are only silence and black void without our senses. But it is all a preparation for something greater. It is a mockery if a redwood tree exists for centuries and we seldom make it to one century. Not to have a life after this one would be like fire fighters rushing into a burning house to rescue the furniture and leaving the residents to perish! Our lives are wonderful and full of potential that can only be realized by an extension of this life.

    b. Brings hope for life. A village played a trick on an alcoholic one night hoping to scare him out of his drinking. They carried him out to a grave in the cemetery dug for a service the next day, thinking that waking up there would shock him. Next day when he awoke, he looked around and said, "Well, here it is resurrection morning and I'm the first one up!" We dream and hope for eternal life to continue to share love with our family and friends and enjoy existence. It would be cruel simply to perish and dash the hope that is in all of us.

    c. Brings justice to life. Life is unfair. Some innocent children may live a few years of abject poverty and torture, while some very cruel persons may have a very comfortable and long life. Heaven is necessary to bring justice to the universe. Otherwise life can be a cruel hoax for many.

Peter Pan said that death would be an awfully big adventure.

G-9. When Church Becomes Too Familiar

Purpose Statement: *When worship and being a Christian become so routine they lose meaning, we need a shot in the arm to revitalize our faith.*

Think about the pictures on the walls in your home. You probably hardly ever notice them anymore. They are so familiar you do not even pay attention to them. We say the Lord's Prayer and when we are done we may not have thought of the meaning of any of the words. We sing most hymns without paying attention to the words. We come away from the worship experience not having really worshiped at all. The letters to the churches at Sardis (Revelation 3:1-3) and Laodicea (Revelation 3:14-16) hit the nail on the head. Sardis is dead and needs to awaken, and Laodicea is neither hot nor cold. John wishes they were "one or the other."

   a. Danger of falling into ruts.
      1. We don't even know sometimes that we have lost the vital spirit of our faith. Until someone tells us we may not even think about the fact that we are going through the motions, and the meaning of what we are doing has evaporated.
      2. We don't care because ruts are very comfortable. By renewing our faith we may be challenged to sacrifice or serious change. *Status quo* never disturbs us. We can go on sleeping.
      3. We become apathetic. This could be the deadliest sin of the church. Not knowing and not caring leads to a church that is dying and full of dead members.
   b. Getting out of ruts.
      1. Try new things. This is one good reason to learn new hymns: the words are fresh and we pay attention. Altering the worship order or creating new elements to aid our worship could wake us up.
      2. Take control. In the last analysis, it will be up to each individual to do something about it. No matter what

changes the preacher may bring to the worship experience or church activities, each member is on his or her own to take control.

G-10. Kissing: The Holy Kind

Purpose Statement: *It wouldn't hurt to have a sermon concerning how we should show affection in the church family. This is another area where a "happy medium" seems necessary: some, but not too much.*

A short blacksmith acquired a new girlfriend who was very tall. Pondering how they could kiss, they hit upon the idea of his jumping up on his 500-pound anvil so their lips would be on the same level. Soon after he was following her around the town inquiring when they could kiss again and she kept saying, "Not now, later." After a while he commented, "If there isn't going to be any more kissing, I'm going to put this anvil down." When my wife saw the sermon title she asked, "Is there any other kind?" Others might ask the opposite, "Is there a holy kind?"

   a. Affection is important. In a great many churches there is a whole lot of hugging going on. The congregation seems very warm and friendly, as it should be. Judas greeted Jesus with a kiss, albeit in a traitor's act. However, it still indicates that kiss greetings were common. Jesus told Simon that the sinful woman kept kissing his feet when Simon did not even greet him with a kiss (Luke 7:36-45). Romans 16:16 admonishes Christians to greet each other with a "brotherly" or holy kiss. 1 Peter 5:14 indicates we should greet one another with a kiss of Christian love. We need these signs of affection. Unfortunately, the persons in our society most in need of love are the least likely to get it.

   b. It must be appropriate. We have all heard church members say they don't care for kisses and even clergy have been accused of making greetings that are "too friendly." It can be a serious problem for certain churches or church members. Related to the subject is the frightening issue of "inappropriate touching," including children. Jesus took up the little children and "placed his hands on them" (Mark 10:16). Each of us had better resolve some clear guidelines for the show of affection.

c. How do we determine that? It is imperative that we get to know our friends quite well in order to assess their likes and dislikes in displays of affection. Occasions may arise (perhaps provoked by a sermon like this) where it can be discussed and guidelines can be established. Given our culture, we always have warm but safe greetings to fall back on: a broad smile, a kind word, or a good handshake.

H.

H-1. Good God Or Perfect Book?

Purpose Statement: *We need to do what we can to resolve the problem of a Bible that sometimes makes God out to be cruel and unreasonable and by doing so gives permission for our irresponsible behavior.*

a. Perfect book and good God. The ideal is to have the Bible perfect and true in every word, and to have God be perfect in every way. And that is the way most persons casually assume. The Bible is the greatest sacred literature of all religions. We Christians know this to be a fact even though we are biased in our perspective. When we compare the great moral and ethical teachings concerning human behavior with the sacred writing of other religions, the Bible is head and shoulders above the rest. What the Bible reveals about the wonder and greatness of God, no other literature can match. Besides the Bible witness, no Christian will argue with the idea that God is perfect and good. So what is the problem?

b. Perfect book or good God? The fact is that we cannot have both. We must choose to believe either in a perfect book and a vengeful God, or else in a book that has errors and misunderstandings and a perfect and loving God. The simple reason is that the Bible attributes some very "unChristian" behavior to God. God strikes persons down cruelly for reasons for which we would never condemn someone. God kills Uzzah for trying to prevent the covenant box or ark from falling, a very harsh punishment for someone trying to do good (1 Chronicles 13:1-11 and 2 Samuel 6:1-9). God not only wants the Israelites to destroy the Canaanites (Joshua 11:1-20 is a good example), but also joins in the slaughter. Acts 5:1-10 is another story of God's excessive punishment for a sin. This list could go on. It is not sufficient to say we just don't understand God's ways. That is a cop out. Unfortunately, it helps people justify wars, capital punishment, and other crimes.

    c. Good God. We may all want to opt for a good God and thus a book that has some human mistakes and human misunderstandings concerning God. I consider it blasphemous to make God vengeful. Jesus speaks of God's love over and over again! He says we know how to give good gifts to our loved ones, and how much more God will give us good gifts (Matthew 7:11). 1 John is effusive in describing God's love (4:7-21). Don't make the Bible into God. It is not always inerrant in its ideas of God, but it does point to a perfect and loving God.

H-2. Can You Squeeze A Dinosaur Into Your Bible?

Purpose Statement: *It is a sad state of affairs that two wonderful disciplines, science and religion, are at odds with one another. A sermon of reconciliation is mandated.*

We have a history of animosity between science and religion. Religion is fearful that science is proving some theological tenets wrong and setting up an encouragement for atheism. When religion retaliates, science loses respect for religion. A classic example ensued when Galileo proclaimed the earth was round and not the center of the universe, not even the center of the solar system. Pope Urban threatened Galileo with torture if he did not recant (*The Making of the Modern Mind*, by John Randall, p. 235). However, the conflict that disturbs the conservative church the most is the threat evolution seems to be posing to creation, as Genesis apparently understands it. Three statements may be in order as an effort towards resolution.

    a. The Bible is not a book of science. The Bible is not interested in science, but rather it is concerned with religious ideas. We're mistaken if we think the Genesis writers were concerned with everything being created in six days. That was not important to them. What mattered was that there was a God responsible and God had plans for you and me. Many Christians are not aware there are two creation stories in Genesis. The first story, found in 1:1—2:4a (denoted by the use of "God"), was written about 850 B.C. and describes the process as having the animals being created and then people, the way science tells it. The second story, found in 2:4b-25 (denoted by the use of "Lord God"), has a person created before the animals. When considering the matter of time, the first story does not have "days" being created until the fourth day. Couple that with the idea that for God a thousand years could be compared to a day (Psalm 90:4 and 2 Peter 3:8) and you see that time was relative.

b. Scientists are theologians. Since scientists are studying God's creation, the universe, I consider them to be theologians. They are in the process of seeking to understand how God worked in the past and is working today through natural laws. Not everyone in the science community recognizes God in the process, but many do. However, all of them are learning about God, whatever they think.

c. Theologians should be scientists. Many of the early scientists were, in fact, clergy or studied to be clergy. Clergy of today, if they are serious about knowing God, should be part-time scientists. I find science to be exciting and the more I know about the universe, the more wonderful God and creation seem. God works by evolution. If we eliminated evolution from the historical process, we would take the heart out of astronomy, geology, anthropology, biology, botany, and other scientific fields. Creation did not end with "six" days (however many eons that represents), but is still in process.

H-3. Censored!

Purpose Statement: *The church has always wanted to do something about excessive violence and sexual content in the entertainment industry, but has felt inhibited by the stricture against censorship. What can the church or Christians do?*

Censorship is perhaps the dirtiest word in our language. Feelings run high against censorship, and the church's concern regarding certain social problems has been severely curtailed. No doubt, the most flagrant act of censorship in scripture was King Jehoiakim's burning of the scroll that Jeremiah wrote containing God's message (Jeremiah 36). God instructed Jeremiah to sit down and write the message all over again and tell the king he would suffer severe punishment for his censorship. Next would be the censoring of Peter and John (Acts 4:18-20), a common experience in the early church. Some important thoughts on this matter must be seriously considered.

    a. Censorship can't be done. The concern is over the infringement on, or eroding of, our right to free speech and expression. History gives us ample examples of governments denying free speech, which is sometimes the people's only recourse to getting heard. Free speech is a basic and precious right that must be protected.

    b. It is already done. Censorship is practiced in our society in many ways, and often with full approval. We are not allowed to slander other persons without expecting a lawsuit. We cannot make obscene phone calls. We cannot expose ourselves on the street. Television is monitored — a little. We cannot phone in a bomb threat to schools or business places. Certain pictures and words are kept out of the papers. We cannot cry "fire" in a crowded theatre. There is no end to the ways we already censor free speech and expression. We simply label it something else: selection, prioritizing, regulating, etc. It is still censorship.

    c. It must be done. Because people are not responsible and mature in their judgment, society necessarily must censor.

James 3:1-12 reflects on our problem of irresponsible talk and behavior, saying how difficult it is to control immature people. Society must exercise controls or we have chaos. It is either censorship or anything goes. Freedom of speech is not the only right. There is another right that is vital: the freedom not to be hurt, insulted, or embarrassed. Our freedom of speech ends where someone else's freedom from abuse, offense, or injury begins.

d. It must be done responsibly. If I cannot make an obscene phone call that offends another person, why should I be allowed to broadcast through the media the same offensive subject matter? Just as a person's very life hangs by the fate of a jury's decision, we can have responsible and controlled censorship without fear that we will lose our basic right to free speech.

H-4. We Have Met The Monster And It Is Us

Purpose Statement: *Each of us must make a careful and continual examination of our lives to see where we need to change.*

Clichés such as "We are either a part of the solution or we are a part of the problem" are not without their important truths. Pogo once said something like, "We have met the enemy and it is us." The classic statement on this issue comes from the Sermon on the Mount, "We are not to judge others. Before tackling someone else's sin, we must remove the log from our own eye" (Matthew 7:1-5).

a. We blame others and that's okay. While Jesus said not to judge others, we need to spend some time interpreting exactly what that entails. Some have offered a helpful idea by suggesting the word, "condemn." We may judge others, but not condemn them. In fact, we must judge others. Certain actions, attitudes, and behaviors are judged to be wrong for all of us. When you see an adult beating a child, you pass judgment by saying that is wrong. Those things you know are inappropriate for you are likewise inappropriate for others, barring any unusual extenuating circumstances. You judge the behavior, but not the person. Someone might be doing something very wrong, but that doesn't make her or him a bad person. We cannot condemn people or claim to know the "state of their soul" or their relationship with God. Anyone committing a bad act may still be overall or generally more loving and caring than we are.

b. Just remember our part in the problem. It is legitimate to criticize others; however, we are probably due for inspection ourselves. We ought to develop a checklist of questions to ask ourselves in order to expose some needed changes. For example:
   1. Do we leave the shopping cart just anywhere in the store lot?
   2. Do we laugh at ethnic jokes?
   3. De we drive too fast, endangering others?
   4. Are we noisy neighbors; is our dog a noisy neighbor?
   5. Do we cheat on taxes?
   6. Are we cheerful or rude to clerks and others we meet each day?

The questions could number in the thousands. We could begin and end each day with a personal checkup.

H-5. Some Are More Equal Than Others

Purpose Statement: *One of the responsibilities of the Christian is to love the "unlovables."*

Jesus says this several ways, but one passage is particularly pointed. Luke 14:7-24 tells us not to be proud. When invited to a dinner, do not sit in the best seats as if you thought you were important, but take the humble seats. However, the more relevant parts of this teaching are verses 12-13 and 21-23 where we are instructed to invite the poor, the disadvantaged, and those who are usually left out, rather than our friends and the rich.

a. Discrimination is widespread. There is a variety of people we revere and reward and certain others that we are repulsed by or at least reject. We use superficial values to judge some individuals as special and worthy of extra attention and accolades, while others become untouchables. Among many others these include:
   1. Wealth: We lavish special attention on the rich. We want to know them and have them know us. Wealth and power and influence go together and we want to associate with these kinds of folks.
   2. Appearance: The most obvious way we discriminate is by selecting features we find more pleasing and then rewarding these "beautiful" persons with special treatment. On the other end of the spectrum are the ugly and unsightly whom we shun. Many, many sociological studies clearly bear this out. We have lifted up one form of beauty to measure everyone by.
   3. Race: Related to appearance, but distinct in itself, is racism, one of our serious social problems.
   4. Personality: We have certain personality traits that are popular and others unpopular. Along with the above and other values, these traits determine employment, promotion, marriage patterns, elections, etc.
b. Discrimination is devastating. Jesus had good reason for his instructions in the scripture noted above. This social ostracizing seriously hurts the people whom we deem as outcasts and treat shamefully. They become depressed; they can become severely antisocial; sometimes they get a gun and shoot others; and occasionally they commit suicide.
c. Discrimination is prohibited for the Christian. Jesus said we must love those who need it most instead of giving all of our love to those who are petted and privileged. I once had an elementary school teacher tell me about a very attractive little girl in one of her classes who very lovingly befriended the unpopular classmates. She herself was very popular and her association with the unpopular children did not cost her any popularity with the admired group.

One or two years later, another teacher said the same thing about this girl. This kind of attention to the disadvantaged is our special assignment as Christians.

H-6. Is There Any More Bible Around?

Purpose Statement: *Why is the Bible bible and are there any more sacred writings that reveal truth about God?*

We believe that the Bible reveals what God is like and how God intends us to live. Do any other sacred writings provide a revelation of God? For scripture readings, the minister could compare some of the best of writings from Hinduism, Islam, Buddhism, Taoism, etc., with the teaching of Jesus. Although I am biased, I find the teachings of Jesus far, far superior to all other sacred writing.

    a.   Sacred literature of other religions. Each religion has its sacred writings. Every minister should be familiar to some extent with those writings: The Koran, the Bhagavad-Gita, The Book of Mormon, etc. Each of the sacred works of other religions has serious obvious flaws, but each has some truths to be considered. However, none of them offers anything that needs to be considered in addition to our Bible.

    b.   Apocrypha. There are fifteen books included in the Roman Catholic Bible that Protestants leave out most of the time. There are additional apocryphal works around, but they are mostly fanciful and add nothing new or of significance.

    c.   Secular literature. When considering the sacred writings of other religions, I believe there are secular writings that are superior. Some great novels, plays, and works of non-fiction have much more to offer in the way of revealing God and God's world. We wouldn't call the material "bible," but we can use it for preaching and teaching, as no doubt most of us do.

    d.   The Bible according to you. In closing, one could elaborate on the way the Bible is read by many folks — by seeing it lived in our lives. We study scriptures and try to live according to the truths we read about God. This is the Bible for some persons who otherwise are unacquainted with scripture.

H-7. King James: The Version Jesus Used

Purpose Statement: *Every Christian needs to be familiar with the various translations of the Bible to some extent: why they exist, why some are better than others, and for what reasons.*

We have probably begun to move beyond the point where most Christians believe a certain translation of our scriptures is right and proper and the others are bad. However, there must still exist some confusion over the wide variety of versions. Church members might find it helpful to know the strengths and weaknesses of the different translations in order to select the one or two or three they prefer for different reasons.

    a. King James. A brief history of the preservation of scriptures and different translations up until and including the time of the King James would be interesting. A Freudian slip causes some to refer to this version as the Saint James. It is interesting to note that when it first appeared in 1611, it was criticized as sounding like a newspaper and that it denied the divinity and messiahship of Jesus. When sailing for the new world in 1620 the Pilgrims refused to carry the KJV with them. It took fifty years for it to be accepted. (*The Bible in the Making*, by Geddes MacGregor, p. 147). Wycliffe, the first to translate the Bible into English, so incensed people for that act that they dug him up about forty years after his death and burned his body. Tyndale, for translating the Bible into English, was strangled and burned at the stake in 1536 (*Know Your Bible Series*, Vol. 1, by Roy L. Smith, p. 11).

    b. Other translations. Give strengths and weaknesses of the key translations, especially the more popular ones today: *The New International Version, Good News Bible: Today's*

English Version, and *The Living Bible.* The latter, which is sort of "far out," is a favorite of the conservatives despite their aversion to anything that moves away from the traditional. The key to their acceptance is that it is considered only a paraphrase (you might think about that one a while). For scripture readings, you could read some passages from different versions for contrast.

H-8. There's No Plan "B"

Purpose Statement: *Each Christian should feel that it is up to her or him if Christianity is going to make a difference in our world.*

Many Christians might admit they feel more peripheral than central to the church. They associate; others do the work. Is this a fair assessment of their understanding of their role? There is the story relating how Jesus was met by some angels in heaven who questioned him concerning his success on earth and future plans. Jesus said he left a few individuals to share the good news. The angels asked, "And what if they fail?" Jesus answered, "That's all I have." Jesus sent out 72 followers with a few instructions. He said the harvest was ready, but admitted there weren't many harvesters (Luke 10:1-11).

a. There is no plan B. The timing was bad. Jesus came too early to take advantage of radio, television, videos, or other mass media. Perhaps that was a good thing. Even the books were only awkward scrolls copied laboriously by hand. He chose not to write anything and there is no indication he gave instructions for any of his teachings to be written down. Apparently, from what meager evidence we have, it was only later that some followers felt the urgency to record his history and teaching. Everything depended on a few dedicated individuals who were going to die soon as martyrs. That was the only plan.

b. So now we are plan A. There have only been fourteen ministers in the last fifty years who did not say, "We are the only voice, the only feet, the only hands Jesus has; it is up to us." And now I'm no longer one of them. Any thinking Christian knows what she or he must do. We cannot sit back and let others be the disciples. The potential harvest is vast, and the choice to do something or sit on the sidelines is ours. Most Christians aren't doing much, and probably know more about the characters on soap operas or sitcoms than about the Bible or the teachings of Jesus. And this is all Jesus has?

c. So what's our plan? We can look at the task Jesus calls each of us to as either a dreaded burden or an exciting adventure. Witnessing, praying, financing, teaching, leading, organizing, serving, and so forth can be approached with reluctance, or we can have enjoyment and satisfaction because we use these opportunities to be creative and well organized, doing neat, tidy jobs. The fellowship can be rich as we build beautiful relationships with other Christian harvesters. And there is the deep satisfaction of knowing we are working for and with God.

H-9. Astrology, Flip A Coin, Or Jesus

Purpose Statement: *What criteria do we use to make critical decisions?*

Some things we simply do and neglect to question the procedures. For instance, how many of us have an intentional process for making decisions? When voting for political candidates, when taking a position on a social issue, when making moral choices, or when simply making daily routine decisions, do we have a guide, formula, or set of rules for direction? What are they? How did we arrive at them? Are they worthy? Deuteronomy 4:1-10 is a clear and precise call to understanding God's law and being faithful to it. (In interesting counter-distinction Leviticus 20 is best quietly ignored.)

113

a. Following the crowd or popular opinion? Unfortunately, perhaps too many of us let others do our thinking for us. We are swayed by the common accepted policy or lifestyle of our peers or the group with which we identify.
b. Feelings? This may mean we have no orderly worked-out plan or any aids to decision making. It is carelessly random, inconsistent, irresponsible, and dangerous.
c. Whatever brings the most happiness? Hedonism is always a popular alternative, not to mention that it is egregiously self-centered.
d. Just take care of "number one" ... and help others when it is not any trouble? This method or philosophy is little different from the last *modus operandi*.
e. A carefully defined set of principles? What are those principles and where did they come from? (You can elaborate on the following.)
   1. The Bible?
   2. The Ten Commandments or Beatitudes?
   3. "Reverence for life"?
   4. Jesus' summary of the law: "Love God and love your neighbor as you love yourself!" (Mark 12:28-31)?
   5. "What would Jesus do?" I despise clichés, but this one bears our most serious consideration. I have preached incessantly that we must read and reread Jesus until we know the spirit of Christ so thoroughly we will instinctively know the proper moral response to almost any situation.

H-10. Drug Deal At The Cross

Purpose Statement: *Perhaps something as prevalent as drug problems in our society should not go unnoticed and unmentioned from the pulpit.*

There are related concerns surrounding drugs in our lives: the use of illegal drugs, overuse of prescription drugs, and some legal drugs that are more abused and devastating to our society than illegal drugs. This focus is well within the church's concern.

a. Jesus says "no" to drugs. An intriguing story at the cross, found in Mark 15:21-23, recounts how Jesus was offered wine mixed with a drug called myrrh before his crucifixion. Perhaps we would be guilty of reading too much into the event, but some suggest the drug was offered in order to dull somewhat the suffering involved in dying on a cross. This possibility is interesting because Jesus turns down the drink. Are we adding more than is really there if we believe Jesus turned it down because he did not want to cloud his mind or lessen the pain and suffering? Somehow it adds additional meaning to an event that certainly needs no further enhancement. Jesus would neither invite martyrdom nor in any way be masochistic. However, it seems consistent with his life that he would never take an easy way out. I hope this isn't suggesting we encourage heroics.

b. Paul says "yes" to drugs. In 1 Timothy 5:23 Paul advises his friend to drink some wine occasionally for some persistent stomach ailment. In this case it would not have been grape juice (see message M-9!), for it was in some sense medicinal. If there is benefit to alcoholic drink today, then it certainly belongs under prescription orders to avoid abuse. There are folks who worry about overmedicating or becoming dependent upon drugs, and consequently they may overreact by denying themselves helpful medication. Safely prescribed medicines are important and advisable; yet, the caution against overdependence is certainly commendable.

c. We say "yes" and "no." As mentioned above, properly prescribed medications are appropriate, and we might safely assume that Jesus would approve. On the other hand, "recreational" drugs are anathema under all circumstances. And for the truly prudent and sensible individual, that would include tobacco and alcoholic beverages because

115

of their severely destructive nature. Jesus (Matthew 18:6-9) and Paul (1 Corinthians 8:9-13) would seem to advise accordingly.

I.

I-1. Baal: The 2003 Edition

Purpose Statement: *Baal was the chief rival to God during Old Testament times. What would be the chief rival to God today?*

For much of Old Testament history, Baal was the one Canaanite god that was the greatest disruption to the Hebrew's true worship of God. There was syncretism as some Baal values and practices slipped into the Jewish faith and from there into Christianity (more than we want to know). The prophets fought one long, continuous battle over centuries to rid Judaism of Baal influences. One example is found in Judges 2:11-14 where the Baal influence has angered God. The classic moment came with Elijah dueling 450 Baal prophets on Mount Carmel for survival rights (1 Kings 18). If we were to consider the "baals" of today, what would they be? Actually not much different than the Baal of old! Baal was ...

a. The god of sensuality. As a fertility god, the rites and ceremonies surrounding Baal naturally took on a sexual flavor with licentious dancing and related activities. One doesn't need to look around very long today to recognize sex as one of our major preoccupations. We advertise with it; we entertain with it; we talk and joke about it; we obsess over it. Sex is meant to be beautiful. However, we degrade it by using it in vulgar commercialism and exploitation. Just as food is important and can be very enjoyable, we can become addicts and pig out. So, sex is idolatrized in our society. Baal is alive and well.

b. The god with no moral values. Baal religion had no concern whatsoever with morality. Baal devotees were not admonished to live good, kind, peaceful, or just lives. You could cheat in business, abuse your family, or insult and harm your neighbor. The only repercussions might be someone retaliating in anger. Baal and Baal priests did not care. We also slip some in attention to moral details today. We

117

smile jokingly at highway speed laws. We "extort" legislators to ignore making sensible laws by threats to nullify them by our violations. We find ways of distorting and destroying family values. In some circles the word "morality" is outmoded and ridiculous.

c. The god of good times. Baal lured the Jews away from God with the promise of having fun and constant celebration. Pursuing selfish ends and encouraging greed are popular pastimes in a nation with excess wealth and resources. Too many Christians would choose attending a football game over Sunday worship. An evening at a casino is preferable to the meeting of a community organization concerned with social values. Watching *Friends* on television is more popular than a lecture series at the local college.

The Old Testament prophets are rolling over in their graves.

I-2. Staking Out Your Donkey On Friday

Purpose Statement: *What day is the Sabbath and what do we do on it?*

Exodus 20:8-11 is the fourth of Ten Commandments (as is Deuteronomy 5:12-15). It speaks of a two-fold purpose for keeping a day, or the seventh day of the week, as holy: to worship God and to rest. Not a few Christians may be hazy or confused about how we keep this commandment.

a. Which day is it? Some "people of the book" (the Old Testament is considered scripture by Christians and Jews) celebrate the Sabbath on Saturday, or Friday night through Saturday. People who are Seventh Day Adventists and Jews (who are apparently growing in numbers because we see a lot of them out playing golf on Sunday mornings) claim the seventh day or Sabbath is Saturday. They observe this last day of the week and consider Sunday only another weekday. Quite a few Christians consider Sunday as the

Sabbath claiming Jesus rose on Sunday and the first Christians began to gather and worship on this day, thus creating a new holy day or changing its place in the week. You might consider several angles in preparing this sermon. As the calendar has changed over the centuries when days were added or dropped, was the order of the days, Sunday-Monday-Tuesday-etc., carefully preserved? Is Old Testament law still binding for New Testament people (not eating pork, animal sacrifice, etc.)? Is adhering to the seventh day legalism missing the real purpose? Jesus said the day was made for us, not us for the Sabbath (Mark 2:27). Because certain people have to work on Sabbaths (physicians, firefighters, law enforcement, etc.), should we have different Sabbaths to accommodate them? Could we conceive all days as being holy and appropriate for worship and rest? I am only asking questions; you answer them.

b. What should we do and not do on it? Jesus has some comments concerning this when he and his followers were criticized for Sabbath activities (Luke 6:1-11 and Matthew 12:1-14). He suggested it was appropriate to heal and save animals from ditches on the holy day. The secret, no doubt, is to understand the reason for a Sabbath. We need to fulfill the purpose and not the legal requirement. We must make sure our worship is real and our rest is truly refreshing and renewing. The story is told that the Pharisees would get around the stricture of the traveling limit on the Sabbath (only so much distance "from your property" was allowed; any more was work) by staking their donkey (their "property") at the limit before the Sabbath started if they wanted to travel farther than the limit on the Sabbath. Then on the Sabbath they could walk to their donkey and then walk again that far beyond the donkey never traveling farther than the limited distance from their property. Do we find creative ways of circumventing the real purpose for the Sabbath? If so, we are not cheating God, but ourselves.

119

I-3. Does The Devil Make You Do It?

Purpose Statement: *Who is responsible for the temptations we face?*

Matthew 4:1-11, Mark 1:12-13, and Luke 4:1-13 report the Devil tempting Jesus at the beginning of his ministry. Our lives seem to be filled with temptations; food, sex, fame, wealth, indolence, and a host of other desirables reach out and beckon us. To have temptation necessitates having a moral order where there is a right and a wrong. To be tempted means feeling desires to do the wrong. Who is responsible for these temptations?

a. The Devil? As is so often true in our scriptures, we have here another example of hyperbole for the sake of emphasis and remembrance. There is no such creature in a red suit with horns and a tail, despite the fact that so many Christians speak of the devil as an actual person. It is amazing we haven't grown theologically beyond such childlike concepts. Two ways the devil can tempt us are totally superfluous. The devil puts temptation in our path? No, our natural environment confronts us with lots of good food to eat and beautiful things to crave that are out of bounds. We don't need the devil for that. The devil puts desires in our minds? Again, "no." When confronted with hard work or an unpleasant task, it comes naturally to want to be lazy. There is no need for a devil.

b. God? Nor can we blame God. James 1:12-13 clearly states that God doesn't tempt us. God has created a world where it is possible to have temptations (see C-1 for related ideas!), but doesn't step into history and place specific temptations before us. The prayer, "Lead us not into temptation," does not mean that God will lead us into temptation unless we make it a point to ask God not to. It means help us through these temptations.

c. Ourselves? The buck stops here. The only one responsible for my temptations is I. I am not responsible for placing them before myself (unless of course I do go looking for trouble), for nature does that part (James 1:14-15). I am responsible for how I handle the temptations. That goes for you too.

I-4. Guess Who's Coming To Dinner

Purpose Statement: *Just how open is our life to Jesus and are we missing anything?*

Zacchaeus only wanted to see Jesus and had no intention of anything beyond that. Jesus was on his way to the fateful week in Jerusalem (Luke 19:1-10). Zacchaeus heard Jesus would be passing through Jericho and climbed a tree to see him. The crowd anticipating Jesus must have been enormous. The whole event was a great experience, and poses the question: "What could happen if we went out of our way to see Jesus?" The amazing thing is that many Christians think they have climbed that tree and had that dinner when they haven't.

    a. Jesus invites himself to dinner. His invitation to us comes first. Our invitation to him comes second, if at all. God seeks out each and every person with a standing and permanent invitation.

    b. Zacchaeus welcomes him. We sit down with Jesus at church, but do we invite him home for dinner? Every Christian needs to ask whether she or he has gotten well acquainted with Jesus, his life and teachings — even the "born again" and "saved."

    c. It meant cleaning house. That dinner experience changed Zacchaeus into a new person. He cleaned house. He gave half of his possessions to the poor and more if there was any incident where he might have cheated anyone. We wonder why we might not respond to Jesus' invitation to come to our home for dinner. Is it because we must clean house and change our behavior, involving sacrifice and discipline?

    d. Salvation came. It seems so strange that we would hesitate to accept salvation by not inviting Jesus to dinner. This is

121

probably so because we think we have salvation already on our own terms. We go to church and are, within the acceptable limits, good persons. What more can Jesus ask?

I-5. Back When Snakes Had Legs And We Were Ignorant

Purpose Statement: *A sermon to straighten out some inconsistencies and misleading thoughts perceived by Christians concerning knowledge, work, and eternal life.*

Genesis 3 carries a fascinating story about man and woman falling into sin. The snake tempts Eve, who tempts Adam in turn, to eat from the tree of knowledge. The snake's punishment is to lose its legs and the people's punishment is now to have to work for a living. Finally, precaution is taken so that people will not win the "live forever" prize. Before trying to provide an answer to the mystery, one could ask three intriguing questions.

   a. Did God really not want us to know right from wrong? Being able to distinguish right from wrong is a part of what makes us human. Innocence is only a virtue if we choose good over evil. Not to have the choice between right and wrong is to be a little automaton or robot. We would have no free will and never be able to grow and mature. Surely, God wants us to have discerning minds, capable of moral choices and solving problems.

   b. Did God really not want us to work? The alternative to work is to lie around indolently, growing fat and lazy and useless. We need tasks to develop a sense of purpose, achievement, dignity, and usefulness. Work solves problems and causes us to mature. Everything we do involves work: learning to walk, read, and relate to others.

   c. Did God really not want us to live forever? To live a brief lifetime and die without fulfilling our fondest dreams and potentials would be cruel and unjust. Some believe that Jesus bought eternal life for us. I prefer to think Jesus

122

revealed it to us. Take your pick; either way, God wants us to experience salvation and eternal life.

d. What then is the purpose of this myth? In the light of these three mysteries, what do we make of this Genesis story? Of course, the story is a myth and not history. It seeks to explain God as the author of knowledge, work, eternal life, and all other good things. It is a parable and not intended to explain 100 percent of the elements of the story. After all, God should not be thought of as being anthropomorphic. God did not "walk in the garden," change his mind, and have trouble foreseeing the future. The religious truth of this parable is that God wants us to appreciate and use knowledge and work. Both are good and gifts from God.

I-6. Does Christianity Take The Fun Out Of Life?

Purpose Statement: *The title says it all: Does Christianity ask us to give up pleasures and good times, and thus fill our lives with boredom and drudgery?*

I strongly suspect that there are many potential Christians, and even some Christians, who assent to the above question. Could there be very many who avoid church because they believe the answer to this question is "yes"? Luke 5:33-35 and Matthew 11:18-19 give us a vivid contrast between two lifestyles: that of John the Baptist who practiced an austere and disciplined life, and Jesus who enjoyed life and was called a glutton and a wine-drinker. Does our faith drain the joy out of life?

a. Yes. The popular quip, "Everything fun is either illegal, immoral, or fattening," is a truism for some individuals. Certainly, Christianity calls for denial (giving up things which are harmful, even if pleasurable), sacrifice, service, discipline, and possibly attracting persecutions. "Selling all and giving to the poor," "Going the second mile," "Taking up our cross," and "Drinking of the same cup (suffering)" are intimations of serious expectations. Would-be followers of Jesus found the demand too difficult, and the followers did suffer hardships.

b. No. The general philosophical approach to life in Eastern religions is one of asceticism, seeing life as negative and the physical world as something evil from which to escape. While Christianity has its monastic side, mentioned above, there is a stronger tendency to celebrate life and the physical world as a special gift from God to be enjoyed aesthetically (Psalm 8). We believe that our faith should affirm life and the best in life: peace, satisfaction, health (through discipline), joy, hope, and the greatest positive, love. These are greater gifts than anything that we "give up" for the faith. In most cases, it is a choice between short run and immediate gratification (in many ways destructive), and long term, deeper satisfaction. It is sort of like candy now to decay the teeth or vegetables which bring better health and with it much more enjoyment from life.

I-7. A Word To The Wise About Strange Words

Purpose Statement: *What about "speaking in tongues"?*

Not too much is made over this issue anymore, and yet it does surface occasionally. I served a church where some outside "saints" came in for a revival-type event and spoke in tongues, claiming that it was evidence of the presence of the Holy Spirit. The corollary being, "If you don't speak the language, you don't got the spirit." The experience at that event left me cold. The speaking in tongues was simply a very few syllables repeated over and over. Paul seems to have the definitive biblical word (although pretty much ignored) on *glossolalia* in his comments in 1 Corinthians 14. Though Paul seemed to tiptoe around the issue very carefully so as not to hurt anyone's feelings or throw cold water on their enthusiasm in the faith, he put the phenomenon down as somewhat less than classy and a not very helpful practice. Paul claims he speaks in tongues (v. 18). How much store do you place in that when he also says women should keep quiet in church (verses 34 and 35)? Five scripture ideas must be discussed, plus one additional consideration.

    a.   Speaking in tongues is not really for public worship; it is a private thing (vv. 2-4). It is unintelligible to others and useless in gatherings. Do it in private.

    b.   Speaking intelligently is far more practical and reasonable than in tongues (vv. 5, 19). Paul insists that speaking must be intelligent and edifying (understood).

    c.   Some people will consider you crazy (v. 23). Even if it were real, it is embarrassing to others.

    d.   Unless someone can interpret what you are saying into the vernacular so that it can be understood, be quiet (vv. 5b, 28). There never is anyone there who can interpret, and yet they will persist in speaking in tongues.

    e.   It seems to be something that can be turned on and off at will, not Spirit-moved (v. 27)! Only two or three should speak, and only one after the other in order. Also, the fact that they shouldn't use tongues unless it can be interpreted is further evidence that it is controllable and perhaps contrived.

    f.   It seems to be a copycat experience. Paul doesn't say so, but we never see it happen until someone has observed it in another person. It would appear that the Spirit won't move anyone to speak in tongues. Only other persons can lead you into the experience.

I-8. Was Jesus An Uncle Tom?

Purpose Statement: *Are the teachings of Jesus too passive and unworkable?*

Another message, L-2, raises the concerns that Christianity is seen as too effeminate and better suited for women and children, a serious mistake. I believe the definition of an Uncle Tom is one who acquiesces into a doormat, not wanting to disturb the *status quo* or rock the boat. *Uncle Tom's Cabin*, written in 1852 by Harriet Beecher Stowe, is a misunderstood anti-slavery novel.

    a. Uncle Tomism is not confined to an ethnic thing. The connotation we unfortunately attribute to Uncle Tom is that of a person who is not willing to stand up and be counted. It connotes one who says all the things we want to hear and not what we need to hear. Uncle Tom is as passive and inoffensive as possible. This bowing and scraping to ingratiate can be found in most relationships where there is difference of status: employer/employee, sergeant/private, teacher/student, and so forth. This is the negative side.

    b. Uncle Tom is a timing thing. The positive side is that the posture, sometimes mistaken for backwardness and fear, may be appropriate at one time and not others. Uncle Tom, of the novel, was in a position where resistance at the time was useless. The numbers and power were stacked against him. It was timing also for Jesus. He left the city at night (Matthew 21:17) during Holy Week so as to avoid arrest. He wasn't running away, but timing his arrest, trial, and death for the right moment.

    c. Uncle Tom was not weak. I understood his character in the novel to be a loving and compassionate person. Under horrible conditions of slavery, where persons have no dignity and respect, Uncle Tom did not hate or seek retaliation. He was kind and generous and peaceful. The general usage of "Uncle Tom" is a misnomer. It would be more accurate to say "Uncle Clarence Thomas" today to imply what we generally mean. It takes great strength of character to be loving and forgiving in situations such as Uncle Tom found himself. Uncle Tom today might be a DuBois, Malcolm X, or Martin Luther King.

    d. We shouldn't confuse Uncle Tom and Jesus. One could say Uncle Tom tried to live as Jesus taught, but not that Uncle Tomism was anything like the epitome of Christianity. Turning the other cheek and loving enemies (Luke 6:27-29) is not weak, but requires courageous strength.

(Note: African-Americans have a legitimate concern over the novel because it is not possible for a white person, such as Stowe, to appreciate fully a slave's experiences and feelings.)

I-9. Is Your House Haunted?

Purpose Statement: *No plan for preaching is complete without an occasional sermon on fear.*

Halloween is not a bad time to preach on fear and what it can do to us as well as what we can do about it. Sandwiched between the bravery of Shadrach, Meshach, and Abednego (Daniel 3) and Daniel's facing the lions (Daniel 6) we find an amusing account of fear. King Belshazzar (Daniel 5) hasn't been a very good person and a warning of his punishment comes in the form of a disembodied human hand writing a message on the wall. Of course we would not be frightened, but he becomes very unnerved. Each person may have her or his own kinds of fears.

a. Fear of things. Phobias are unreasonable or excessive fears of certain objects or conditions: spiders, snakes, heights, crowds, water, close spaces, etc. We can still have fears that are not phobia strength, but that still bring displeasure to our lives. Occasionally, extended exposure over gradual time can help us overcome these.

b. Fear of death. Psalm 23 affirms the faith that though we walk through the valley of death, we will not fear it. Much of the central theology of the Christian faith is concerned with giving us hope for life beyond death. The Easter message is a year-round truth to sustain Christians who face not only their own death, but also that of loved ones.

c. Fear of God. Psalm 111:10 tells us that fear of God is the beginning of wisdom, an idea reflected in Proverbs. Generally, it might be a good idea to use the word "reverence" for "fear" when referring to God. Unfortunately, there are some passages that mistakenly attribute some frightening actions to God. 2 Samuel 6:1-11 relates how David was

127

bringing the Ark or Covenant Box home when God struck down Uzzah for doing what most of us might consider a good deed. Understandably, it put the fear of God into David and he decided not to bring the Ark home. This kind of fear of God is uncalled for. It is respect, awe, and reverence that are appropriate. We are to love, trust, and depend on God.

d. Fear versus concern. You might say these are two separate subjects. In the minds of many, they are related. Concern is a "healthy fear" or respect that causes us to be cautious and play safe. Concern causes us to pray for and advise loved ones traveling on the highway, etc. Worry is bad, concern is good; it may not be that easy to separate them in our emotions.

e. No more fear. 1 John 4:18 tells us that perfect love eliminates fear. If we have love or a healthy spiritual life, we have much less reason to fear, as well as the resource to overcome our fears.

I-10. Why Do Lions Eat Lambs?

Purpose Statement: *Why is there so much violence and suffering in the natural world?*

Message C-1 deals with evil and suffering for humans in this world. It seems fair to ask why a loving God allows violence and suffering in the animal kingdom as well. The answers in the previous message do not seem applicable to this topic. We have to find other explanations and this is probably the hardest question for which to find answers. Most persons will find it difficult to see violence to any kind of animal life and not be uncomfortable. I hope that most individuals prefer the image of the peaceful kingdom that is often portrayed on Christmas cards nowadays — lions and wolves hanging out with lambs and bunny rabbits. This ideal world of peace is described in Isaiah 65:17-25. Verse 25 says that in this new earth and heaven the carnivores and herbivores will live in peace together. There will be joy and full enjoyment of life. If this is the ideal image, how can we justify a loving God creating fear and pain for animals in a violent nature?

    a. It must not be as traumatic for animals. Animals do not have loving relationships, hopes and dreams, and enjoyment or appreciation of the beauty of the world as we do. (We speculate this is true, anyway.) Consequently, their death is not as great a loss as ours. Perhaps, their sensitivity to fear and pain is not as sharp as ours is.

    b. Death is inevitable anyway; this is just another kind.

    c. One hopes there is also some kind of life after death for animals. It could be implied in the Isaiah passage cited above where a new heaven is envisioned where lions will eat straw instead of lambs.

    d. It does not give us permission to be cruel. The foregoing discussion is only theoretical; this point is practical. We should never be cruel to the animals because:

        1. They should not have to suffer any more than they already do in nature.

        2. Being cruel to animals does something to us in terms of desensitizing us to the beauty and wonder of God's world.

        3. Cruelty to animals may say something important about our own character. Adults noticing children being cruel to insects or animals should regard that as a red flag. That child may have serious problems or be headed that way. A person who can feel pain upon seeing an animal hurt has a loving and sensitive spirit.

J.

J-1. Made Anybody Uncomfortable Lately?

Purpose Statement: *God's word is not always popular and can make us feel uncomfortable. Are we sharing God's uncomfortable word with others?*

God sent out all of the great prophets and religious leaders of our Bible with messages that irritated those in power, and at the least, made them uncomfortable. Amos, Moses, Jesus, Paul, and a host of others were disliked and unpopular. Jeremiah was a classic example (20:1-10). Pashhur, one of the Temple priests, had Jeremiah beaten and chained (vv. 1, 2) for saying things God asked him to say. It made those in authority upset with Jeremiah, and the entire population (v. 7) even down to his close friends (v. 10) ridiculed and whispered against him. Yet if he didn't speak up, withholding it was like having a fire inside him (v. 9). He didn't want to, but had to speak for God.

   a. Some people make us feel uncomfortable. I mean for righteous reasons. What they say or what they stand for makes us feel ashamed by contrast. Remember how Paul said we could heap coals of fire of shame on their heads if we do God's will. The question is to determine if we are one of those making others uneasy, or are we one of the uncomfortable ones? Examples of what we need to be protesting when we speak for the right would include:
   1. When someone confesses he steals little things at the workplace, we don't let it pass quietly.
   2. We do not listen to gossip, but try to stop it.
   3. We let others know we don't tolerate racial or ethnic jokes.
   4. When someone mentions he drives too fast, we find a way to show how we feel.
   5. If a clerk gives us too much change, we return it.

The list is endless and we have opportunities every day to make a witness.

    b. We don't want to be one of them. It makes us uncomfortable to make others uncomfortable. Why?

        1. We don't want to lose friends.

        2. We also know that we too are sinners.

        3. We are not always sure of the right way to speak up. It must be done with humility. Jesus could be condemning of actions and attitudes and yet he ate with sinners. It cannot be done in a condescending, self-righteous way. Should the pastor speak out to correct behavior?

We need to ask ourselves, "Have we made anyone uncomfortable lately?"

J-2. Does Our Church Have A Narrow Gate?

Purpose Statement: *Has our church discovered the narrow way Jesus spoke about?*

    a. What is this narrow way Jesus said was so important (Matthew 7:13-14)? My favorite way of illustrating this concern is using the analogy of the compass. There are 360 degrees or directions or paths a person can take, but only one true north. (Put aside the technical facts that there are two norths, and the directions are infinite; we are only speaking two-dimensional.) If you have one certain destination, then that one single path or true north is the only way to reach your goal. All other 359 directions lead elsewhere. If you choose one of them either you never reach your goal or you will have to renegotiate your directions at some point. God has one true way in comparison to many other possibilities that are not God's preference for us.

    b. Have we found it? This pattern may be applied to all aspects of our lives: our moral choices, our career choices, our choice of who our spouse will be (or not at all), and

131

down to even how we are going to use the next hour of our life. In many cases, it will not come down to one right choice and 359 wrong choices. It is not that simple. It may be a matter of several good choices — some better than others — and many bad choices. In some instances, it can conceivably be a matter of only one good or right choice. Have we found the narrow way? As Christians, are we significantly different from the world? Or are we indistinguishable from everyone else?

c. Has our church found it? Jesus said the narrow way was hard. Does our church make being a Christian and/or a church member seem easy or difficult? Does our church preach a lifestyle that calls for discipline and sacrifice, as well as comfort and satisfaction? Are we occasionally disturbed and challenged by sermons and church class discussions, or is it only an atmosphere of peace and good times? Does our church resemble a congenial social club? Are we encouraged to stretch and grow?

J-3. The Church Should Mind Its Own Business!

Purpose Statement: *What constitutes the appropriate concerns for the church?*

No one would argue with the notion that the church needs to define clearly its bailiwick of concerns and be true to its task. Whatever the business of the church is, we must be diligent and enthusiastic in our work. The argument comes at the point of what constitutes the proper concerns of the church. If we can agree that everything is the church's business directly or indirectly, we will disagree on how we approach that business.

a. Two trends: saving souls or social action. It may not be fair, but I will generalize and over-simplify the issue and claim there are two ways of approaching the church's work. One trend favored by conservatives or evangelicals would be to "preach Jesus" and get people saved. If we do that,

132

the saved will go out into the world and make decisions that will make our communities more peaceful and just. Another trend espoused by liberals is to discuss serious social issues (gambling, abortion, etc.) and then to organize campaigns, protests, letter writing, and other demonstrations to bring about change. To be fair to the conservatives and to complicate the matter, conservatives have in recent years seen the light and gotten into social action also.

b. Saving souls hasn't worked. That is not to say saving souls isn't important or that we don't do it. However, it is to say that this method of Christian witness doesn't lead to effective social change. Consider the existence of slavery in our country. There was a lot of preaching of hell fire and damnation and saving souls, but nothing done about slavery. It took social action before civil rights took giant steps and partially restored people's freedom and dignity.

c. That leaves social action. Amos was a great social activist who saw corruption and injustice in society and demonstrated and protested against it. Any of several passages will illustrate this, but chapter 8 is nice. Amos saw the needy and poor being trampled and could not remain silent. The church is mandated to speak out. We must discuss and debate until we reach a consensus on issues (and no issue is out of bounds!), organize, and demonstrate.

J-4. Religion From A Safe Distance

Purpose Statement: *A sermon attacking our efforts at trying to be a Christian with minimum effort.*

Have some of us been able to make a commitment to Christ, become a church member, and consider ourselves a Christian, and still been able to avoid the difficult parts of the faith: discipline, sacrifice, struggle, change, challenge, etc.?

a. We know the challenge of Christianity. Romans 12:1-3 makes the commitment to Christ sound very rigid and difficult. Words like "living sacrifice to God" sound very ominous. It means becoming a new and different person. It means sacrificing things we desire and enjoy. We must give up this world's ways and accept a disciplined lifestyle. There may also be times when the going will get tough. Although Christians seldom experience anything that could be called persecution today, it is not out of the question. The disciples fled when Jesus was arrested. Two followed at a "safe distance," but either denied knowing Jesus or simply did not speak up.

b. We avoid and postpone commitment. Some persons are not ready to make the kind of commitment they believe being a Christian requires. They refuse to join a church or avoid attending to escape responsibility. The hen said to the pig, "Let's surprise our farmer owner with a nice breakfast of ham and eggs." The pig replied, "That's easy for you to say. For you it is an offering; for me it's total commitment."

c. Finally we find an easy way of doing it. Some Christians are able to find the secret of "partial commitment" or, as I like to call it, "making their peace with Jesus." They have discovered ways of being a Christian while avoiding real commitment. It's much like a student in class who raises his or her hand for all the easy questions so as not to be called on for the hard ones. Or a committee member who will volunteer quickly for two or three easy tasks knowing it will reduce the chance of later being asked for the rough jobs. It is analogous to the circus elephant that fell off her stool during a performance. It unsettled her and the trainer found it impossible to get her to do the trick of sitting on the stool again until one day she started doing her trick with no hesitation. The sudden change puzzled the trainer until one day he noticed the elephant was not actually sitting on the stool, but only crouching over it. Have we found some "easy way outs" for serving Christ?

J-5. Finding God In A Quiet Universe

Purpose Statement: *Most Christians would admit to difficulty in experiencing the presence of God in their lives.*

If it is true that it is not always easy to feel God's presence, and if it is important to know God in some relationship, it behooves clergy occasionally to preach on finding God. Job 23 speaks for many Christians if they are honest about their concerns. Verses 2, 8, and 9 express the frustration of where and how to find God. Perhaps since we have created a very noisy world for ourselves, the noise crowds God out. We have traffic noises, radio and television on constantly, and what passes for music playing all around us. Some of us are afraid of or do not know what to do with uncluttered quiet time. If God seems too silent for us, we may have been given a clue as to how to find God. An amusing passage comes from Revelation. Chapters 6 and 7 describe the opening of the seven seals of heaven. There are galloping horses, violent earthquakes, and shouting people. And after all of the commotion, the seventh seal is opened (8:1) and there was "silence in heaven for about half an hour." That says volumes. Tradition tells us we find God three ways (someone could come up with a doctrine and we could call it, perhaps, the trinity):

    a.   We find God in the creation. I am overwhelmed with God's presence in the wonder of the universe. Psalm 8 expresses it well. What astronomy tells me about the staggering grandness of space with its quiet galaxies and stars leaves me awestruck. Both in space and time the universe is amazing and yet very quiet for us. We are told, "Be still and know that I am God" (Psalm 46:10). The wonder and magnificence of nature should lead us to worship. The beauty of flowers, clouds, mountains, oceans, canyons, and animals should leave us in awe. The joy of music, the love of people, and the comfort of good food and rest should stir emotions of profound thanks and appreciation. The little boy was impressed with the nature guide's ability to see animal tracks, seeds, and wonders of the woods. So he

asked, "Can you also see God?" The guide answered, "I can't help seeing God."
b. We find God in Jesus. We all know the revelation of God found in the life and teachings of Jesus.
c. We experience God's spirit within us. 1 Kings 19:11-12 tells us God wasn't found in the roaring fire, or stormy wind, or crashing earthquakes, but in the soft whisper or still small voice. Through prayer and meditation, we find that quiet, inner voice, that warmth and peace, that stirring of the heart, the feeling of love that is God.

J-6. Is The End Near And Should You Worry?

Purpose Statement: *Jesus' second coming is a fascinating and popular subject for many Christians. It is imperative to preach on this very prominent New Testament concern.*

(Another title might be "No End In Sight!") Conservative Christians make this subject central to their preaching and so we assume it is of vital importance to their lives. Because of the nature of the subject, it warrants a more comprehensive approach rather than the selection of isolated verses as I have done here. However, I think the conclusions offered here are valid. At least three things may be said which are relevant to the eschatological event and when it will happen.
a. We can't know. Jesus tells us we cannot know when such an event will happen (Matthew 24:36). Yet the conservatives are busy searching the scriptures for signs. They have so many and they change so often when the time doesn't work out. I remember my conservative friends making much to-do about the second coming scheduled for forty years after the reestablishment of Israel which happened in 1948. You do the math. I was told this was the final piece to the puzzle. The problem is if we knew the time, we could theoretically wait until just before the event before getting ready. Jesus foiled this plan by saying we must

136

always be ready (Matthew 24:44). Many of the signs are taken from the most confusing and least understood book in our Bible, Revelation.

b. It has already happened. Jesus said that it would happen before some of those he was speaking to had died (Matthew 24:34). If he meant us today, then he thoughtlessly misled everyone for 2,000 years. One thought: Jesus has already come twice. Another thought: the event has already happened for everyone who has already died.

c. It shouldn't matter. Knowing a date for a second coming should never make a difference in our life. We should live our best every day regardless of when or if. Would you want your child to be good because he or she didn't know when Mommy or Daddy was coming home, or to be good because that was his or her nature? Some are wont to say, the second coming should be preached to give a sense of urgency to our conversion or commitment to Christ. I would answer that we already have a more realistic and imminent event to give us that sense of urgency — our death.

J-7. Is Church Dangerous?

Purpose Statement: *Is there anything unpleasant or inconvenient about going to church?*

Cars cause twenty percent of all fatal accidents; seventeen percent of all accidents happen at home; fourteen percent of all accidents happen to pedestrians on the street; sixteen percent of all accidents happen in air, rail, or boat travel. Only .001 percent of all accidents occur in church. Yet, one could say that it is dangerous to go to church.

a. The danger of persecution. Jesus warned his followers that they would suffer and die for their faith and service to him (Matthew 10:25-30). What they had to say would so disturb those in power that the persecutions would be fierce. I doubt that the sins of today are any different: it is the

137

same message we have to offer for the same offenses. (See messages E-4 and L-3.) The fact we don't suffer the same persecutions is probably due to the sophistication of our listeners today. Our suffering for serving Christ would come in subtler ways today; if you call losing your job, for instance, instead of being thrown in jail or beaten, subtler. At least, most of us don't worry over the suffering and death the disciples experienced happening to us. The dangers are mostly of another kind.

b. The danger of being disturbed. I have always said there are two kinds of sermons: one that comforts and inspires, and one that disturbs or challenges. Many Christians could do with a serious self-examination. We need to be shaken out of our complacency and smugness. We are sinners and need to repent and confess. At times we need to be the tax collector in the Temple who beat his breast asking God to be merciful because he was a sinner (Luke 18:13-14). Our sins should disturb us into humility and repentance.

c. The danger of being challenged. Jesus said the harvest was ripe and ready for the workers. The tasks awaiting Christians who are willing to serve are daunting and overwhelming. A rich ruler came to Jesus and Jesus asked him to sell all his possessions and give it all to the poor (Matthew 19:16-24). He did not anticipate the danger of losing everything when he came to Jesus. The challenge was too much.

If we think that church today will not cost us anything, it may already have cost us more than we think.

J-8. Am I My Butterfly's Keeper?

Purpose Statement: *How we care for the animals may tell us a lot about our love and sensitivity for other people.*

One of my favorite stories concerns a time long before automobiles, when a clergyman rode into town one stormy night and pulled up to an inn. When inquiring about accommodations, the innkeeper asked his denomination. The clergyman asked if that really mattered. The innkeeper said, "Yes, Presbyterian ministers want a nice room and good food; but a Methodist minister is more concerned about his horse." The clergyman said, "I am a Presbyterian, but my horse is a Methodist."

a. What? Romans 8:22-23 tells us that *all* of creation "groans" with pain. The world is a difficult place filled with much suffering (see sermon I-10). We must share the planet with a great variety of other creatures and plants and often that other life is destroyed by our "progress." Environmentalists tell us that we are determined to have "progress" at any price, and our environment is being destroyed. The natural world is shrinking as the concrete and steel encroaches. Animal habitat is disappearing at an alarming rate.

b. Why? Why should we care or do anything? In the first place, respect for God and appreciation of God's creation is enough motive to call us to careful stewardship. There is much beauty and wonder in nature. Animal life is precious and a sensitive person hurts whenever a life is needlessly destroyed. I hate to drive at night because the insects swarm towards the headlights and perish on the windshield. One day, a monarch butterfly hit the windshield. When I stopped the car it was still alive but injured. I did not know whether to put it out of its misery or lay it along the side of the road. The next Sunday I preached on "Requiem For A Butterfly." Someone who tortures animal life and feels no pang is missing something vital and needs help. Reverence for life is love for God.

c. How? Never needlessly take life. Seek to preserve life; we need the other creatures absolutely. Build shelters and birdhouses; plant trees and seed plants. Don't lightly dismiss the thought of becoming a vegetarian (and not only because it is the healthy lifestyle). Whatever side you come down on this issue, a serious Christian considers all options carefully so as not to overlook what might be God's way.

J-9. Start Quoting God Accurately

Purpose Statement: *Integrity demands that we are careful and honest with our use of scripture to quote it accurately.*

Statements such as "You can make figures say anything" or "You can find a Bible verse to support just about any position" are very familiar. As regards the Bible, it has, in fact, been used to justify everything from most wars to segregation and slavery. It is used to prove capital punishment is both right and wrong. Can it be both ways? There is a humorous book titled *Nice Guys Finish Seventh* by Ralph Keyes, which cites the many misquotes that most of us take for fact. For instance, apparently the famous manager did not actually say, "Nice guys finish last." The serious question is: "Just how much is our Bible abused by misquotes or improper interpretation?"

a. Of course we have to read the Bible. We must become familiar with passages and background so as to be accurate and understand the meaning or various meanings. We hear, with good reason, "never take a quote out of context" *ad nauseam.*

b. Seek other sources. It pays to use Bible aids, study books, or guides in order to make the proper rendering clear. With careful analysis, the passage may not say what we want it to say, but we cannot be less than honest.

c. Focus on Jesus. I consider this to be vital for the Christian. Where contradictions arise in scriptures, the ultimate judgment rests with what Jesus said. The Old Testament tells us, "An eye for an eye," for example. However, Jesus actually quotes this law and immediately contradicts it by saying, "Do not take revenge" (Matthew 5:38-39). Also, if one listens closely, one will hear the conservatives quoting Paul much more often than they quote Jesus. With the liberals, the tendency is just the opposite; Jesus is quoted much more often than Paul.

d. One interesting test for accuracy. It is not proof of truth, nor obviously is it the only test. But it is a good one. If you

140

can honestly say, "I don't like what I am hearing," but you believe or accept it anyway, that is a good indication you are playing fair with the Bible! Jesus may seem to say something you don't agree with. Some persons would try to "interpret" the passage to make it say what they want to hear. Do you?

The world is always in a mess and Christians are not in agreement with solutions. The secret is for us to read God's word and get it right.

J-10. Will Your Bones Dance Again?

Purpose Statement: *Is there any evidence of eternal life or heaven?*

Ezekiel 37:1-14 gives us a vision or analogy of resurrection where dry bones are brought to life again. Christians who are honest, while having a faith in Jesus and his teaching regarding a life after this life, still harbor occasional doubts. Most persons would be interested in discussions regarding evidence of eternal life. (See G-8 for reasons why eternal life is necessary and K-9 for what heaven must be like.) Among the possibilities, the following are some convincing evidences:

a. Nature. We see evidence of a type of resurrection in nature. Though not technically dead, trees go dormant in winter and revive in spring, flowers die over winter and return in spring, caterpillars are transformed into butterflies, etc. There is a law that states nothing is ever lost in the universe. Matter is being changed constantly, either into other matter or into energy. Speaking egocentrically, it would seem that the very best, the human soul and mind, would not be lost after a few years of life. Our minds give meaning to everything else in our world. Without our minds and souls to appreciate the world, what are beauty, joy, physical laws, and mathematics? Is that which can best appreciate the universe and give it meaning destroyed?

b. Potential. We are growing and developing animals. We mature in wisdom and virtue. We become more understanding of ourselves and our relationships with others over time. Could that potential be destroyed short of goals or ends, making us like ships setting sail on the seas never to reach any port?

c. Love. The relationships we build grow into a love where two become one. We would die for loved ones and friends because they are our very lives. Only a cruel God would allow this kind of love to grow towards perfection and die. If there is no eternal life, our loves are ended tragically forever!

d. Resurrection. Anyone questioning the resurrection of Jesus is missing a critical fact. Whether it was physical or spiritual (there is ample evidence suggesting both), some very real experience changed the disciples from frightened people who denied knowing Jesus into courageous persons who were willing to die for the privilege of telling others about the resurrection.

K.

K-1. Holy Smoke

Purpose Statement: *What are the ingredients of true worship?*

Other messages (G-2 and G-9) in this book deal with the issue of letting worship lose its meaning for us. Perhaps an examination of what constitutes real worship is needed from time to time. Isaiah 6:1-8 gives us a dramatic look at one person's exceptional worship experience. The Temple was filled with smoke for Isaiah. Is that the difference? If the church filled with holy smoke when we worshiped, we would all go out and become great prophets. But it doesn't and we don't. How do we experience the holy smoke?

    a. Intention. Isaiah had to have wanted to experience the Holy Spirit to go to the Temple. We need to ask the reason why we go to church. Chances are much greater that we will experience God's presence if that is our goal.

    b. Preparation. Hebrews in Old Testament times sang hymns on their way to the Temple. Preparation is so important. Great concert pianists must prepare assiduously. Successful athletes practice regularly. What do we do? Probably stay up late Saturday night (into Sunday morning) at a party or watching television. Our vision at church the next morning may be blurry, but not because of holy smoke. We must prepare our minds long before we get to church.

    c. Extension. If worship is real for us it can happen anywhere, and does. Isaiah was the biblical exception. Most of the great worship experiences of the Bible happened away from church: Moses in the desert, Paul on the road, Jesus in the garden, Ezekiel outside (11:13-14), Paul and Silas in jail (Acts 16:23-26) — the list is endless. I'm not suggesting we don't worship in church. I'm only saying it starts there and continues wherever we might be.

    d. Practice. Real worship makes us follow through with holy living. Isaiah heard God calling and he responded by saying, "I will go, send me" (6:8). The famous analogy of the Dead Sea and the Sea of Galilee is *apropos* once more. The Galilean Sea had an outlet and was fresh and full of fish. The Dead Sea had no outlet and harbored no life. If worship is real we go out and serve.

K-2. That's Blasphemy!

Purpose Statement: *The definition of blasphemy is making mocking, slanderous, or vulgar speech concerning God or sacred things. We sin in many ways, but it would seem that we would not be guilty of blasphemy. And yet there are ways we can offend God.*

It would be more appropriate to say that God is saddened or disappointed with us at times, but never offended. Matthew 12:30-32 poses an interesting problem with an interesting possible solution. Jesus tells us that the only unforgivable sin is blasphemy towards God. From all that Jesus teaches us about God, it would seem that God forgives all sins when there is sincere contrition and penance. Thus the only unforgivable sin would be the refusal to accept forgiveness, which is to maintain a broken relationship with God, which in turn would be true blasphemy. I would think the following beliefs about God would constitute blasphemy.

    a. Believing God to be unjust. Christians believed God supported slavery and the KKK and white supremacy. We sometimes act towards the poor as if they deserve their poverty as God's punishment. After the burning of black churches a few years ago, a letter appeared in the paper claiming it was God's judgment. Europeans felt justified in the eyes of God to take the land from Native Americans.

    b. Believing God to be ridiculous. Burning animals in worship or witches in superstition, assuming God's approbation, makes a mockery of God. Searching for a secret code God supposedly hid in the scriptures concerning eschatology makes God seem petty and foolish.

c. Believing God to be cruel. Believing God wanted the Canaanites slaughtered or wants us to practice capital punishment or go to war makes God out to be very cruel.
What we believe about God determines our spiritual state and our behavior.

K-3. Multiple Choice: Sapphires Or Wisdom?

Purpose Statement: *One of the disciplines of a concerned Christian should be continuing education.*

Life is a multiple-choice activity. We are faced with decisions every day, and it would seem the best preparation for making the best possible choices would entail being well educated. The political vote, handling finances, moral decisions, questions raised by our children, etc. are examples of difficult questions we must answer or decide. The beautiful story of Solomon asking God for wisdom instead of wealth (1 Kings 3:1-14) should be a lesson and an inspiration to all of us. I suspect that given the choice, most of us would choose wealth over wisdom. The book of Proverbs, which was naturally attributed to Solomon, stresses the importance of wisdom, and even becomes emphatic on the matter (1:1-6, 22-33 and 8:1-36). Explicitly, wisdom is better than jewels (8:11) and everything else for that matter. Wisdom must be high on the Christian's priorities, but I don't see that as a reality.
a. What is wisdom? It is both knowledge and common sense. Both are derived from conscientious study. Intelligence helps, but wisdom is attainable despite intelligence. Education is critical and should never end. Education is attending classes of all kinds (and there is a great variety available for us today), reading the Bible and reading in general, attending Sunday school, keeping up with the news, having creative hobbies, thinking and meditation, getting acquainted with God's world, using libraries, educational television instead of *Miami Vice*, asking questions, doing new and different things, challenging one's mind

145

with puzzles. In other words, having a voracious appetite
for knowing. Scientists tell us that our minds do not slow
up with age as much as we think, but rather because we
tell ourselves they will or we simply let them.
  b. Why is it necessary? 1) To enjoy life more. 2) To have a
      better life. 3) To be able to know and do God's will. 4) To
      be mentally alert and healthy as we age. 5) (There's more.)
  c. Why not? 1) We are suspicious of education. 2) We are
      complacent and happy with things as they are (but we're
      not). 3) We don't have confidence in our capacities. 4) We
      do not like learning (when we get into it in earnest, we
      grow to enjoy it thoroughly).
Jesus said to be wise as serpents (Matthew 10:16).

K-4. When Christianity Gets Unreasonable

Purpose Statement: *There are religious concepts that seem imprac-
tical or foolish. What do we do with them?*

We are asked to accept on faith what we cannot understand.
However, it would be a mistake to believe just because we find it
written in the Bible we should follow blindly. One example should
suffice to show the ridiculousness of this possibility. Leviticus 20:9
counsels that anyone who curses his parents should be put to death.
This is not something we should accept by faith. The question remains as to what to do regarding unreasonable dictums in scripture. 1 Corinthians 1:18-31 speaks of the Christian message as seeming to be foolish.
  a. Some illogical statements are true and may never be un-
      derstood. One reason why this is true is that the universe is
      too vast and complicated and not everything can be known
      or understood. Another is that we cannot know completely
      the mind of God. Examples of this kind of subject would
      include space, eternity, God, and the wonder of love.
  b. Some illogical statements are false and must be ignored.
      Along with the example cited above from Leviticus, there

are many dangerous ideas that we would do well to ignore: a devil in a red suit, a punishment of eternal burning hell, an anthropomorphic God, killing people in war and by capital punishment, etc.

c. Some seemingly illogical statements are logical and on further investigation we find it is possible to understand them. 1 Corinthians 3:2 and Hebrews 5:12 state we are not always ready for meat or solid food and must be fed milk only. It is only as we mature in our faith and theology that we can begin to see that some aspects of what we considered unreasonable, are actually very logical and practical. That the earth was round and "floating" in space no doubt seemed impossible to early inhabitants; but when we know the physical laws behind the phenomenon it seems sensible. Vaccinations, where we give individuals a dose of the disease, seem unreasonable until explained more thoroughly. The cross, as Paul says, is foolish to the uninitiated. As we mature we see the power of the cross as well as pacifism and turning the other cheek. Meekness and forgiving enemies are practical and sensible when we become knowledgeable of God's ways.

d. There is a key to unlock the mystery of illogical statements. A two-step plan should always be used to unravel the seemingly unreasonable. Every idea must be consistent with the life and teachings or spirit of Jesus! God gave us minds and we should use 1) logic and 2) prayer to probe every irrational appearing Christian idea, comparing it to Christ, until the sense is made clear or its falseness is known.

K-5. It's Not What You Got — It's What You Do With It

Purpose Statement: *Stewardship is using wisely what we have.*

Matthew 25:14-29 relates the story of three workers being entrusted with the employer's property, each being given a portion to take care of. Two of the workers used the property wisely and one did not. For the purpose of this sermon it would have been far better if Jesus had told the story with the person getting the least portion doing better with it than the ones who got more. Let's imagine he did tell it that way and it was changed in the process of recording and recopying over time. The point is still abundantly clear either way: the way we use what we have is important.

a. We've been given different talents. One of my professors at Duke reminded me how hard it is to fill a cup to the brim when holding it under a faucet running at full force. Then he said some of us have spoons. The world wouldn't function well if we all had the same talents. We need the variety for the complexity of life.

b. How much isn't important. We delight in measuring talents and abilities. We shouldn't. Some talents considered lesser are just as important as the glamorous ones. We complain and clamor for more or greater talents, while not using what we have. There are wonderful opportunities that take little talent! In one church I served, one of the members suffered a paralyzing stroke. Several men in the church went over to his house regularly for years to help bathe and take care of him so that he could remain in his own home.

c. Use it wisely. After inheriting my daughter's ten-speed bike, I found it complicated and ended up using only one of the middle gears. You have known folks who cover up seats in new cars with seat covers to preserve them. You're one of them, aren't you! Many persons cover the couch with a blanket to save the fabric and go the entire lifetime of the couch never seeing it. One church member saw students on their way home from school picking the flowers in her yard. I would have rushed out and scolded them. Not her. She went out and visited with them about how nice it was that they appreciated beautiful flowers. She told them that anytime they wanted a bouquet to just knock on her door and she would help them pick some. What a wonderful witness.

d. That's how we get more. The point isn't to get more. The point is that responsibility and maturity bring additional gifts with which to serve: wisdom and increased talent.

K-6. Three's A Crowd!

Purpose Statement: *There are great opportunities for significant personal witness with just one or two other persons.*

We must keep reminding ourselves about just what our Christian business is. It is first to worship and grow spiritually; second, to make a personal witness to others; third, work to build more just and peaceful communities. Regarding the second task of personal witnessing, the important numbers to remember are:

a. One. Jesus always stressed the value of every person, and was particularly concerned about "these little ones." The parable of the lost sheep (Matthew 18:10-14) emphasizes the preciousness of a single person, no matter who that person is. Jesus tells of a woman who celebrates over finding just one of her lost coins (Luke 15:8-10). The angels will rejoice over one saved sinner (Luke 15:10).

b. One on one. Our task is to be role models by who we are and what we do as we go about our Christian witnessing. Just being kind and loving, and thinking of others, will influence someone or many someones. Guarding against the danger of inappropriate witnessing (see messages C-3 and D-2) we must be salt and light for the world. I've had elderly persons say to me, "God hasn't taken me home yet, so I suppose he (sic) still has a big job for me. I just haven't figured out yet what it is." I tell them the most important task we can do is to love and care for each person we meet.

c. Two or three makes four. Jesus said that where there are two or three gathered in his name, he is there with them (Matthew 18:20). Even with our imperfections and blundering, Jesus is with us and the spirit of Christ can be in us for others.

149

An astrophysicist professor, Chandrasekhar, of the University of Chicago, lived eighty miles from campus. When only two students registered for one of his classes, to the surprise of everyone who expected he would cancel the class, he drove over back roads twice a week in all weather to teach the class. A few years later both of those students won the Nobel Prize for physics.

K-7. Baptism: What's In It For You?

Purpose Statement: *Obviously it is important to preach on the meaning of baptism once in a while, and clear up some important misconceptions.*

Acts 16:29-34 recounts a dramatic baptism in a jail cell at Philippi where the jailer's family was taken into the church. For Protestants, baptism is one of two sacraments: celebrations symbolizing receiving the love and power of God. Many "Christians" who are on the periphery of the church, and seldom if ever attend, desire to have their children baptized. Unfortunately, their reasons are vague and sometimes faulty. But it is a great chance for education and renewal.

    a. What happens at baptism?

        1. Are we initiated into the church? It is a celebration of becoming a Christian and affiliating with a church.

        2. Are we saved? Unfortunately, many people are under the impression that this sacrament is necessary for salvation. That needs clarification. God is not so cruel and unjust to "send someone to hell" for want of baptism. In the case of little children, they are unable even to make the decision or initiate the experience. Would they be lost because their parents didn't see to their baptism? Hardly.

        3. Do we make a recommitment? We probably made a commitment already or we wouldn't be there for baptism in the first place. It becomes a celebration of a decision we made to follow Jesus and become a Christian.

4. Are our sins washed away? It symbolizes the forgiveness of God that is available for us at all times of true repentance. It is not a once and for all proposition. We will continue to need forgiveness.
   b. How should we be baptized?
      1. Method? Given the symbolic nature of the event and the fact that it is not magical, it should be left up to the individual being baptized to select the method that will be the most meaningful to her or him. Some Christians believe there is only one true way (immersion for example) to baptize. We would probably choose to share that other Christians recognize other alternatives as valid.
      2. Where? Preferably it should happen in a church or church gathering. The church family is to be a part of the experience since it is an initiation into Christianity and the fellowship of Christians. Baptism should be recognized as a Christian baptism, and not a Lutheran, Presbyterian, Methodist, etc., baptism.
      3. When? It can be done as an adult when the person is old enough to make his or her decision. Or it can be done for an infant or child when parents make the decision. The child reaffirms that decision when he or she is older and joins the church.

K-8. Spoiled In The Garden Of Eden

Purpose Statement: *Too much ease and pleasure threatens to distort our perspective and warp our values.*

We hear talk of parents indulging their children by catering to their every whim and thereby spoiling them. This can easily happen in a nation such as ours, which has an abundance of wealth. Even adults can be spoiled by having too much too easily.
   a. We should enjoy life. God gave us this wonderful universe full of potential for joy, love, and the appreciation of beauty.

151

At the extreme, we have visions of the Garden of Eden or a paradise, and this becomes a goal for us as we set about fulfilling our dreams. It becomes a partial reality for many, especially in our country where opportunities are great.

b. Too much can be dangerous. If our needs are met too easily and we have an abundance, we can grow indolent and selfish. We begin to vegetate or strive to get even more of the good things.

c. We can become insensitive to the poor. We soon find it hard to identify with the unfortunate majority in our world who suffer privation. Our cocoon existence colors and clouds our vision. We either forget or try to forget the great need that exists.

d. We can forget our need for God. Soon we feel we accumulated all this by our own skill and deserving. We forget the part that others have played in our good fortune. This includes forgetting God. When we have the resources to buy whatever it takes to meet any need, we feel less need for God. It is beguiling, for our need for God is growing and we are unaware of it.

e. Our possessions can take possession of us. The more we have, the more we worry about protecting what we have, and the more difficult it is to part with some of it to help others.

f. Some rough times might be good for us. After being spoiled in Eden, we were put out in the real world to work and struggle. Deuteronomy 8:1-10 describes the forty-year desert experience that tested the people of God. It was a reality check before entering the land of "milk and honey." We need some discipline and hard knocks every once in a while. Jesus spoke about fasting — that's a start. It wouldn't hurt for God to take us for a walk in the desert every so often.

K-9. Gates Of Pearl; Streets Of Gold: Just Hype?

Purpose Statement: *There are conflicting suggestions in our Bible regarding what life after death is like. Some possibilities seem more consistent with a loving God than others.*

The book of Revelation, as a means of giving hope and courage to persecuted Christians, describes heaven in different ways. Chapters 7:9-17, 20:11-15, 21:1-27, and 22:1-5 are graphic descriptions of heaven that must be contrasted with the great number of Jesus' teachings about salvation and God's love and forgiveness. Any sermon on eternal life probably must list options of beliefs held by Christians. I see no reason why the pastor cannot stress her or his opinion as the best among them. When preaching on this subject, the following ideas must be dealt with:

a. The vivid imagery. John, in Revelation, was not the only one to dramatize in glowing terms concerning heaven. Jesus made exaggeration with poetic license common in his teaching in order to help us remember his ideas as well as to drive a point home with special emphasis. His hyperbolized imagery included swallowing camels, camels passing through needles' eyes, plucking out your eyes, tearing down the Temple, bringing a sword to divide families instead of peace, and so forth. Any sermon on heaven and salvation must start by explaining this technique of Jesus.

b. Hell. The description of hell given by Jesus falls under exaggeration as pointed out above. A loving God would in no way assign anyone to an eternity of torture as suggested by a fiery burning hell. The Catholic Church was uncomfortable with this idea and invented purgatory from an obscure passage in one of the Maccabees books found in the Apocrypha, I am told. It was a nice attempt to avoid the unreasonable cruelty of hell. If, as I believe, there is no hell, then what?

c. Salvation or who makes it? Some Christians endorse the concept of a universal salvation where everyone enters eternal life or heaven, and where there is no such thing as hell.

Their argument, sometimes, is that God could never "ultimately" be defeated, as would be the case if some people never made heaven. I like the idea, and perhaps we all enter life after death at different levels prescribed by how we have developed spiritually in this life.

d. Heaven and what goes on there? It would seem more likely, if we enter into eternal life at the appropriate level of spiritual awareness that we have attained in this life, that heaven is a place where we continue to grow and mature spiritually. We "pick up where we left off" in this life even with the possibility of backsliding at times in heaven. We do not just jump from this life into perfection in the next. Heaven must be a growing experience just as this life is centered on our becoming mature Christians. Certainly, it would involve interaction with others — our loved ones, especially — as it does here, only in a spiritual realm. Eternal life would incorporate remorse and penance for our sins in this life before there would be any growth. Jesus' description of an "outer darkness" and weeping and wailing and gnashing of teeth illustrates this remorse.

K-10. Who Are The Real Christians?

Purpose Statement: *Behind the query of who is and who isn't a Christian lies the fundamental question, "What does it mean to be a Christian?"*

The initial inquiry is intriguing if not practical. We live in a full, busy world rubbing shoulders with countless people every day. Once in a while we may ponder who, of all these persons around us, is a Christian, and who is not. Certain lodges and service clubs wear identification pins. In one sense, it is probably a good idea that we are not so easily identifiable! This eliminates some discrimination of treating some persons better than others. We should care for and be kind to all persons and not just Christians.

The critical question is not about the other person, (we shouldn't judge others, Luke 6:37), but are *we* Christian? What would be some of the criteria?

    a. Church membership? Do one or more denominations have a corner on Christians? Certainly some denominations may have a larger percentage of members who may qualify as "Christian," but we will never know which ones. Each has its share of Christians and hypocrites or pretenders.

    b. Certain beliefs? No doubt this is not definitive. Although the formula of "believing in Jesus Christ as Savior" seems plausible, I am going to hold out for the inclusion of some who are not in this fold (Matthew 7:23).

    c. Being born again? Can we backslide? Is it possible we fool ourselves and psych ourselves into believing we have had such an experience? (See G-4.)

    d. Sincerely trying to follow Jesus? I like this one. Jesus told the parable of the two sons asked to go into the field and work and then turns the tables on our expectations (Matthew 21:28-31). Jesus told another appropriate story concerning who was righteous: a Pharisee (a very religious person) and a sinner were in the Temple praying (Luke 18:9-14). Which one was "justified"? We probably picked the wrong one again. We are Christian when we are sincerely trying our best to be humble, forgiving, loving, etc. It is not a state of having arrived. It is a journey.

L.

L-1. The Dragon Who Ate Himself To Death

Purpose Statement: *A sermon recommending fasting.*

Jesus said, "When you fast ..." implying apparently that we should. Because our health is an important concern and because many of us are overeating, occasional sermons on proper diets and exercise seem necessary. If you couple this concern with the story from Bel and the Dragon, it becomes an opportunity also to educate our church members about the Apocrypha (the fifteen extra biblical books used by the Catholics and increasingly by Protestants also). Since Jesus healed we can assume that Christians should be concerned with health. Nutrition and appropriate eating habits seem natural for the Christian regime. One must not pass up the opportunity to warn of the consequences from the other extreme: anorexia and bulimia.

You have my permission to open with my favorite scripture funny line where Daniel has killed the god Bel and the dragon (Bel and the Dragon 1:23-28). The people are incensed and complain to the king that Daniel has slaughtered their priests and killed their god, Bel, and on top of that, "Now he has killed our dragon!" (It is important to use the *Good News Bible, Today's English Version.*) This replaces my former favorite humorous line from scripture, also from Daniel (5:6), where King Belshazzar is so frightened that, I believe the *King James Version* says, "his knees smote one against the other."

In dealing with the importance of healthy repasts one could simply use the three suggestions:
a. The dragon ate hair and tar: some foods are very bad for us.
b. Daniel enticed the dragon to eat: we are surrounded by great culinary temptations.
c. It remained the dragon's choice: it is up to us.

L-2. Women: What Men Need To Know

Purpose Statement: *Men need to consider seriously being more like women.*

One could make a very convincing argument that part of the reason that we say some Christian ideas won't work (turn other cheek, love enemies, etc.) is because usually men have run the world, and these ideas are deemed too effeminate and thus out of bounds for men. At times and in some communities, the church has been seen as only for women and children. Let's examine this further.

a. Men and women's worlds. Boys are made of snails, nails, and puppy dogs' tails. Girls are made of sugar and spice and everything nice. And these views are more accentuated as we grow up. Men are tough, rough, aggressive, competitive, brave, daring, cold, and unemotional, and they are not allowed to cry. Women are sweet, gentle, kind, thoughtful, sentimental, emotional, and warm, and they tend to cry. When Jesus speaks of forgiveness and love and holds up the Beatitudes (Matthew 5:3-12) for the ideal, these virtues do not line up well with the picture of a man's world we just painted. Love as presented in 1 Corinthians 13 is seen as weak. Christian virtues are more like women's ways. I consider this to be a problem of large proportions. I have even heard of Salmon's *Head of Christ* criticized as appearing too effeminate.

b. Women try to emulate men. Women have no problem dressing in men's clothes (the other way around is usually confined to your private room). To achieve equality in society, women unfortunately believe they must adopt men's ways. Men's ways tend to discard Christian softness and gentleness and kindness as signs of weakness and being unworkable. Women seeking to be more like men are giving up wonderful qualities.

c. Men try not to be like women. Because the traditional roles for men are to be the tough, manly hero, men have shunned the feminine image. They call any boy or man acting too much like the traditional women's role a sissy. Gay bashing is a result of this fear men have of appearing feminine. However ...

d. Men need women's virtues and not the other way around. They say if women ran the world there would be no wars. Before we can have a world of peace and justice, men will have to learn there is power, strength, and courage in Christian love and forgiveness; or women will have to gain more control, and those who do cannot give up the gentle virtues.

L-3. Cheer Up, Things Could Be Worse

Purpose Statement: *Could you persevere through serious persecutions?*

That is the question I ask myself with fear and trepidation.

a. Jesus said we could suffer. Jesus described terrible suffering for his followers (Matthew 24:3-14). They would be hated, arrested, and put to death. If that were prophesied for us, would we remain faithful? Think of the early Christian martyrs torn apart by lions. Early Christians had to choose between professing Christianity and risking the suffering of their families, including the children; or denying their faith to save their lives. The church grew rapidly in numbers under this kind of persecution. I remember hearing about Christians in Russia years ago under Communism who risked losing their jobs and homes if they attended church.

b. Could we endure? Even though we may never experience any serious consequences for being Christian, we should ponder the question. However, we may have to endure lesser trials. I have counseled people who risked losing their jobs for taking a stand for justice at work. Could we be faithful in that situation? I know persons who lost friends because of a moral stand. Could we be that faithful? Youth probably experience the greatest peer pressure to violate their principles. The eighth beatitude claims we are blessed when persecuted for our faith (Matthew 5:10-12). Matthew 11:30 says the yoke of Christ is easy. But could we endure?

   c. How can we know?
      1. We prepare ahead of time.
      2. We can do it if we feel the strength of Jesus sharing the burden of the yoke.
      3. We can by practicing on little things. Some wag has said the reward for good work is more work. Jesus tells a parable (Matthew 25:14-30) where two workers were "faithful in little things, so they could be trusted with greater responsibilities." I find two questions intriguing. Is it possible to be faithful in little trials and not big ones? Yes, but you enhance the probability of success in large tests by being faithful in the small ones. Is it possible to be unfaithful in little trials, but still meet the challenge when the larger tests come? Yes, but again, we enhance our probability by faithfully administering small responsibilities.

L-4. Some Exciting Thoughts On Sin

Purpose Statement: *What is sin and how does forgiveness work?*

This message only partially covers the subject. It should clarify some questions on what constitutes sin and what part repentance plays. For instance, when talking about sin, one could mean a specific act, such as shooting someone; or a person could intend sin to refer to a state or condition, such as being in a broken relationship with God. One of the most beautiful acts of forgiveness was Jesus forgiving the woman who committed adultery (John 8:1-11).

   a. Can you sin in the dark? What is considered sin differs from denomination to denomination. For example: one church claims dancing and gambling are sins. The next church will declare only gambling a sin. And still another church will say neither of these examples is a sin. One could categorize sin into two kinds with various degrees of seriousness within each category. For example: there is a sin of ignorance, where the sinner isn't aware she or he committed a sin. Someone could make a racist remark ("They can't help it if they're black!") and not be cognizant it was a racist statement. It is wrong so it is a sin, even though the sinner is ignorant. It is a sin partially because the sinner should know better. So it is possible to be in the dark or ignorant about the sin. Then there is the willful sin, where a person knows it is wrong and does it anyway. Whether a sin of ignorance or willfulness, some sins are worse than others: murder is worse than theft and injuring someone worse than littering.

b. Can a sin that is not a sin still be a sin? Let us reverse the situation of the sin of ignorance mentioned above or do the converse of it. This time we'll say the act is not a sin in the eyes of God. For example, God may not consider dancing wrong at all. However, if people still believe that dancing is wrong and then dance, they have sinned. The dancing wasn't technically wrong, but since they assumed it was, they were willing to disobey God by doing something they thought God disapproved of.

c. Can you enjoy sin more by getting the punishment over ahead of time? This would be considered corrupt "indulgences," where you could pay the priest to be forgiven for sins you were about to commit. This was one of the grievances Luther had against the church in his day. The answer to the question is: "Yes, you may enjoy your sin more by falsely assuming you are already forgiven; however, the catch is that you aren't forgiven. There has been no real repentance." Similarly, Jesus says to forgive someone seven times (any large number) a day if he continues to sin against you and continues to ask to be forgiven (Luke 17:3-4). Forgiveness is possible under these conditions theoretically, but practically, the repentance probably isn't real, consequently the forgiveness never happens.

d. How to sin and still be a Christian. If you tell me I have sinned and I am no longer a Christian, that wouldn't necessarily be true. All Christians sin. That doesn't mean we are no longer Christians. We have simply back-slidden and need forgiveness. A preacher cannot say, "You drink or you smoke; therefore you are not a Christian."

L-5. So You Think You Can't Swallow A Camel?

Purpose Statement: *It is all about priorities: first things first.*

The religious leaders of that day gave new meaning to the words of Jesus concerning the first being last and the last first. Jesus gave one of the sternest scoldings ever when he castigated the Pharisees and teachers of the Law (Matthew 23:1-36). They had either lost sight of what their faith was all about, or finally just didn't care anymore. They routinely ignored the vital aspects of their faith and emphasized the mundane. He called them hypocrites, blind, violent, and tombs, among other things, because their religious practice was tantamount to worrying over swallowing a fly, while inadvertently swallowing a camel. They were certainly guilty of trying to remove specks from the eyes of others while ignoring the log in their own eye. Yet they were very devout and meticulous about the law of God. Given the context, the message would be for the clergy and other church leaders. Practically, it is applicable to all of us.

a. Do we practice what we preach (v. 3)? Do we talk the talk, but fail to walk the walk, as they say today? We can tell others how to do it, but when the church members are in the church kitchen preparing a dinner or out in front of city hall with picket signs, we are home watching the Saint Louis Rams on television.

b. Do we parade our piousness (vv. 5-7)? Do we have any of that self-righteousness about us in which our motives and goals are only to impress others by our saintliness? As a pastor, I never wanted to know how much any member ever contributed financially to the church. I was adamant about this and always made it clear to the persons responsible for handling the money. One day, when the name of a certain family who was extra pious was mentioned, the financial secretary blurted out in anger, "They act so holy, but they give next to nothing to the church."

c   Do we have poor priorities (vv. 23-28)? Do we attend church every Sunday, but forget what Jesus said about leaving our gift on the altar, and going out to reconcile with someone we share animosity with, and then coming back and worshiping (Matthew 5:23-24)? Do we keep the Sabbath holy by resting and not working, then profane the other holy days of the week, Monday through Saturday, by rudeness or dishonesty? There are a great many things about which we know better; when will we do better?

L-6. What To Make Of Ghosts

Purpose Statement: *If our church members think about it, we'd better discuss it. Are there ghosts? And if so, what does it mean?*

Paul said just as there is a physical body in this life, there is a spiritual body after we die (1 Corinthians 15:44). One question we have is: Can we ever see one of those spiritual bodies while we are still here on earth? Those who believe in, or think they have seen, a ghost would say, "Yes." For the disbelievers, I remind you there are at least four *bona fide* ghosts in our Bible.

a.   I don't believe in ghosts. I would like to, but until I see one (like flying saucers), I will remain a skeptic. I will not ridicule anyone who believes in or claims to have seen one; however, I need evidence. It is not important one way or another, or is it?

b.   But the Bible has ghosts in it. Jesus is the best-known ghost. The Gospels have several stories of the resurrection to

162

verify his return. I can imagine an argument raging over whether Jesus was a ghost or not. Some would say no, because he came back to life. Others would say yes, because those who are dead are alive. The appearance of Jesus after the resurrection takes on ghostly qualities. Mary Magdalene did not recognize him outside the tomb (John 20:11-16). He asks her not to touch him (v. 17). He enters a locked room where the disciples were (John 20:19). Two of his followers on the road to Emmaus did not recognize him for quite a while (Luke 24:13-31). If Jesus doesn't qualify, then Moses and Elijah certainly do. Matthew 17:1-8 gives us the "transfiguration" event where Jesus spoke to, and Peter, James, and John saw, Moses and Elijah. Equally interesting is the account where Saul (1 Samuel 28:3-19) first runs all the mediums or witches out of the country and then four verses later asks for a medium to come and help him. Upon Saul's request, she conjures up the ghost of Samuel, whereupon the two visit a while. These ghost stories are hard to dismiss.

c. What would ghosts tell us? It would be wonderful to "pick their brains" for information about what heaven or eternal life is like. I wouldn't appreciate the experience because about two minutes after I saw a ghost, I'd probably be one! If nothing else, if there really are ghosts, they tell us one of the most important things we can ever know — that there is a heaven or eternal life. We already have ample evidence (see, for example, J-10 and G-8), but reinforcement is always nice.

L-7. You Can't Legislate Morality? — Guess Again!

Purpose Statement: *"You can't legislate morality" is the popular phrase used to defeat laws or rules we don't like!*

We find ourselves debating and arguing over laws that affect us. We usually don't care too much about laws, or anything else for that matter, unless we think they affect us and become personal. "Don't infringe on my rights and freedoms!" Some individuals seem suspicious of our government as if it were a dictatorship. They call the government "Big Brother" and warn others about too much control. This never sounds very patriotic to me, and yet it is the "flag wavers" who are the most suspicious. One of the most used arguments by someone opposing a law he suspects might rein in his freedom is to say, "You can't legislate morality." This statement is used to argue over many issues such as gun control, drug abuse, abortion, slower speed limits, etc. The Old Testament gives us the Ten Commandments (Exodus 20:1-17 or Deuteronomy 5:1-22) among many others. Jesus summarized the law into two simple ideals (Mark 12:30-31), yet, though he clearly warned of the dangers of legalism, he would have us live by rules: "Turn the other cheek" and "Give to the poor."

    a.   You can't enforce the law. This is what they mean, but "legislating morality" sounds more charged and pious. The truth, of course, is that we can't enforce the law 100 percent. And laws do not change bad persons into good persons. The accompanying clincher is when the person says, "Remember how Prohibition didn't work?" But Prohibition was a success. (You must see E-10 on this one.) To use this argument is perilously close to extortion: "If you pass that legislation, I and others won't obey it."

    b.   Yes, you can enforce the law. Laws do work, if not 100 percent. A significant proportion of persons do obey. When that number gets low, it is because the law isn't enforced, not because it can't be enforced. Laws do provide a safer society. Laws make a statement about right and wrong. To legalize the drugs that are now illegal would send a message that it is permissible and the erroneous message that it is safe.

    c.   The alternative: Do away with law. "You can't legislate morality" says you won't make people moral. We all know obeying rules because we care for others and want to protect them is preferable to obeying rules out of fear of punishment. But the latter is preferable to having no rules at all. Without laws our world is chaotic.

L-8. Welcome To Judgment Day

Purpose Statement: *Judgment day and getting saved may not be exactly what we are anticipating.*

We need to help church members tweak their beliefs concerning salvation and that pearly gates thing. They may have some misconceptions that will lead to disappointments. But more important, it could make a significant difference in how they conduct themselves in the here and now. I have always been amused by the way Amos describes judgment day (Amos 5:18-20). He makes it sound just the opposite of what we normally expect. The "Day of the Lord" will be sad and gloomy, not happy and bright; it will be like a person running from a lion and getting caught by a bear. Perhaps I should be less amused and more on guard. Yes, I might have lifted the passage just a tiny bit out of context, and some eschatological folks will reprimand me for confusing judgment day and the "Day of the Lord" which they might say is the "great rapture," or whatever. Let's not quibble. The question is: Do we really understand salvation and getting into heaven? Let's look at three assumed assurances:

    a.   Just believe in Jesus. Jesus abhorred legalism and we have made John 3:16, "Whoever believes in Jesus is saved," into a legalism. It makes salvation into a formula. It tends to make everything too easy and routine. Reality is more like John 12:44-48. We must "obey" Jesus and follow his words. I hear John 3:16 everywhere and even see it on banners at sports events. Believing in Jesus means becoming transformed, growing gradually in our faith, and *serving* others. Don't give me the old story that we are not saved by works. Works and faith are inseparable (James 2:14-20). Read Matthew carefully. (Matthew 7:21, 12:33-37, 21:28-31, 25:31-46 or a host of others.)

    b.   God loves us. But we are building our own judgment just as a bodybuilder lifts weights to strengthen the body. We need to build our spirits with love and service. A professor once told his students to grade themselves for the final grade of the class — and he stuck by those grades. Judgment is built in. We are developing our souls for life after death. It is like packing a suitcase for a trip. We mature in our salvation relationship with God through love for others. How healthy will your soul be?

c. We can get right tomorrow. Sneaky as we are, we whisper to ourselves that we can wait a while longer to make the commitment, change our ways, and serve the Lord. God hears us. The practical problem with this eleventh hour approach is not that it can't work, but that it is so much harder to accomplish later. The analogy I like is: We come to a fork in the road and must choose either the path that leads to salvation or the other one. We take the other one telling ourselves we can go back and take the salvation road later. But the paths diverge and it becomes harder to cross over the farther apart they become. And it is a long way back to the fork and easy to get lost. Think about it: Today is judgment day; are you satisfied with it?

L-9. Smile, You Really Are On Candid Camera

Purpose Statement: *We are making a witness whether we know it or not, and whether we want to or not.*

Everyone's watching you! We live in a social world, a house of glass. Our conduct will be observed by everyone we meet — and many we don't. *Candid Camera* was a fun program. It was all about our behavior being observed when we least expect it, and it is. Who's watching you?

a. "Angels unaware" (Hebrews 13:1-2). God sees you. That should be enough. In the sheep and goats parable, whatever we do, we do it unto Jesus (Matthew 25:31-46). The followers of Jesus on the road to Emmaus didn't recognize him at first (Luke 24:13-31). Appropriately or not, I always interpret this event as being able to recognize Jesus or the spirit of God in others. Each situation comedy on television has its version of the person going to an important interview and making a fool of him or herself in the elevator ahead of time. The character doesn't realize, of course, the person on the elevator with him is the interviewer. It is always interesting for clergy to visit with people somewhere, such as on a plane, where people don't know they are visiting with a minister. When they find out, how the conversation changes. Why should it change? It shouldn't matter if it is God, Jesus, angels, or a clergyperson we are talking to. Everyone should command our respect.

b. People who hurt. That thoughtless driver you were angry with may have just lost his son through suicide. The clerk you barked at may be fighting cancer. That stranger on the street you couldn't find time to smile at may have just lost her job.

c. Someone looking for a role model. A while back, a famous athlete said he did not have to modify his conduct and be on his best behavior because he was not a role model for youth. Unfortunately, he did not know that that choice was not his to make. Like it or not, it was an inescapable fact that many youth looked up to him. His only choice was whether he would be a good or bad role model. Our neighbors, strangers, and literally everyone who sees us, may be influenced by observing our behavior. Smile, you are on someone's camera!

L-10. Can You Keep A Secret?

Purpose Statement: *If we are so eager to pass along secrets, why can't we be as excited about sharing our faith?*

When someone asks, "Can you keep a secret?" it is already too late. I know you can keep a secret, but can the people you tell? Mark relates several incidents in the life of Jesus where he asks that no one tell what happened. Here are some examples. Mark 1:40-45 tells the story of Jesus healing a man and telling him not to tell anyone, which is precisely what the man did. He spread the word everywhere. Mark 8:27-30 has Jesus telling his disciples not to tell anyone he is the Messiah. In Mark 9:2-9 Jesus tells Peter, James, and John not to mention the Transfiguration to anyone. Jesus does not always give reasons for the silence. In some cases could it be reverse psychology? No, probably not. But reverse psychology works and I intend to use it on you today.

    a. It is hard to keep a secret. Gossip comes under this category. Four clergy persons were out in a boat fishing on their day off. One said, "We're out here alone; let's each confess one sin to the others. No one will ever know." After agreeing, one said he was a compulsive gambler and no one knew. Another said he kept his alcohol problems well hidden. A third said he once embezzled some church funds. The fourth said he was an incurable gossip and couldn't wait to tell the bishop.

        A man came to the minister and confessed he had revealed a secret entrusted to him and told some gossip. Now he wanted to know what he could do to right the wrong. The minister told him to take a bag of feathers and place one on every doorstep in the village. He returned saying the mission was accomplished. The minister then told him to go out and pick up every one of the feathers — it was a very windy day.

    b. Especially when you are told not to tell. They say when the priest tells the church not to see a certain sinful movie that is the sure way to bolster attendance for that film. Tell a person not to touch something because it is hot or the paint is wet. You probably can never guess what is the first thing that person will do. Remember Lot was told to get his family out of Sodom and for none of them to look back or they would die (Genesis 19:12-26). Lot either neglected to tell his wife, or he told her and she just had to touch the wet paint.

    c. Why is it so easy to keep a secret when you don't have to? Jesus wants us to tell others. We have good news about God's love and forgiveness, the church, salvation, and the teachings of Jesus concerning how to live.

    d. So, don't tell anyone. You can keep a secret, can't you?

M.

M-1. Would Jesus Get A Divorce?

Purpose Statement: *This is a very difficult subject, but there is such a high percentage of persons who are divorced, divorced and remarried, or contemplating divorce, that it merits our attention.*

Surely, many church members are confused over when and if divorce is right. Surely, ministers have had divorced members ask, "Am I living in sin?" The subject is made more difficult because it is hard to understand the position Jesus took. Mark 10:1-12 seems to be Jesus' definitive word on the subject. His position appears to be: There should be no divorce (vv. 8-9), and anyone divorcing and remarrying is guilty of adultery (vv. 11-12). Other addenda would include: a man (sic) who, apparently, has never married commits adultery by marrying a divorced woman (Luke 16:18), and in Matthew 22:23-30 Jesus seems to say nothing to challenge the Jewish tradition of a man marrying his brother's widow. What should the Christian's position be?

a. First, if not totally prohibited, divorce should be an extreme last resort. Jesus stresses the importance and beauty in the rich relationship of marriage where two become one. Divorce reflects failure at some point, and it creates a host of problems, which are especially compounded when there are children. In a day and age when everyone is talking about family values, it is easy to see that greater numbers of divorce reflect not just families with problems, but a society that has serious problems. Divorce destroys potentially beautiful relationships, or more accurately, is the culmination of a destroyed relationship. Currently, we stress exploring all other avenues before seeking divorce.

b. Second, it may be a matter of a "higher" principle taking precedence. There are times when two principles clash and one must choose between them. In this case it would be choosing between the sin of divorce and the sin of people destroying each other in a disastrous relationship. One could, perhaps, obtain Jesus' approval of divorce by some creative interpreting. When Jesus says, "What God has joined together," we could claim a broken relationship was never "joined by God" no matter who said the vows.

c. Third, how do you resolve the problem of a divorced person contemplating remarriage? The reason for Jesus or the church's caution is that at some point a series of divorces and remarriages becomes simply promiscuity. It would seem there is some limit to whether these marriages are real relationships. Unless one has a more creative way of sidestepping Jesus, one may have to say, "It may be wrong, but I am doing it!"

d. Fourth, once a divorced person remarries, the problem shouldn't be compounded with another divorce. The sins of the past are forgiven and forgotten. When people ask me if they are living in sin, I reply that it is a new life from today forward and a fresh start when sins are forgiven. God doesn't want another broken relationship.

e. Finally, as mentioned above, Jesus apparently doesn't condemn widows and widowers who remarry.

M-2. God May Not Even Know Our Country's Name

Purpose Statement: *We have a difficult time understanding that everyone is a child of God and consequently our brother or sister. This is about patriotism.*

The book of Ruth is always interpreted in a personal, one-on-one kind of way. I have never heard it used as an analogy of international relations. Perhaps it is time. Ruth is willing to make a new home with her mother-in-law in a foreign land. The famous first chapter has the marvelous and oft-quoted line, "Your people will be my people." Ruth will adopt Naomi's Israel as her new country. It has nothing to do with turning her back on her own country. It has to do with people and human relationships being far more important than a country. This is a lesson we are far from learning. Colonial powers went into Africa and established "national" boundaries, but to the indigenous peoples those boundaries were artificial and meaningless. So also, the way we have divided up the world is of no consequence to God. The earth is one nation in God's eyes.

    a. We separate ourselves from the rest of the world. They say there are two kinds of people in the world: those who divide the world up into two kinds of people and those who don't — and very few of the latter. We create enemies every chance we get: "we versus them" situations. We create flags and make them sacred in an idolatrous way. This is our flag and it sends the message to the rest of the world that we stand apart as separate and even better people. There are two sides to the coin of patriotism. On the one hand, patriotism means we are united and loyal to each other. The other part of that is we become a clique unto ourselves, and see others as different and suspect. The cliché idea of coming together and becoming united usually means united against others.

    b. Then we want God on our side. After the attack on the World Trade Center, everyone was flying the flag (apparently as a call to war and revenge), and the statement, "God bless America," was seen everywhere one looked. Someone asked the question, "Why aren't we saying, 'God bless the world'?" Because we want God on our side. God shouldn't bless our "enemies."

    c. But God is not on our side. It is very difficult for us to understand that God loves everyone the same. God doesn't want anyone killing anyone else. God doesn't recognize flags or the boundaries of countries. We are children of God, and sisters and brothers to each other — or should be.

M-3. Crying Over Spilt Perfume

Purpose Statement: *Making the best of a bad situation, or picking up the pieces.*

There is no question that Matthew 26:6-13 and Mark 14:3-9 are the same story of a woman anointing Jesus at Bethany, and this is the story we will use. Luke 7:36-39 and John 12:1-8 are probably the same account, only remembered differently. A woman, doing a compassionate deed, poured expensive perfume over Jesus' head, and his followers criticized her for wasting the perfume. They had heard Jesus preach many times about taking care of the poor, and here was such an opportunity of giving to the poor. But Jesus saw a different side of things.

    a. It became a teaching moment. So often Jesus took an incident and elaborated on it to teach a particular lesson. We, like the disciples, have so much to learn, and one of those things is how to use certain happenings to teach or help others.

    b. Jesus avoided hurting her feelings. The woman did a loving act and the disciples' response would seem like a slap in the face. Jesus praised her, saying she did a "beautiful" thing, she anointed his body for death, and it would always be remembered of her! It is important to be sensitive of the feelings of others. Whenever I read this scripture, a story comes to mind about a gracious hostess who, after her guest accidentally broke a piece of her expensive china, in order to put her guest at ease, laughed and threw another piece on the floor, making some comment about it not being valuable.

    c. We can make the best of a bad situation. The disciples were probably right: Jesus' real choice would have been to sell the perfume and give the money to the poor. However, the deed was done, and it was time to make the best of it. We have heard all the sayings: "Make a purse out of a sow's ear," "Get a lemon, make lemonade," "Every cloud has a silver lining," and more. We know what to do; it just isn't easy to know how. When insulted, we can find a creative way to show love. When caught in heavy traffic, listen to tapes or meditate. Each of us needs to work on being more thoughtful and sensitive.

M-4. When Christianity Is Bad Business

Purpose Statement: *To do the moral or Christian thing in some instances means jeopardizing your job, as well as friendships.*

Demetrius, a silversmith in Ephesus, made little silver images of the temple of the goddess Artemis (Acts 19:21-41) and probably of the goddess also. Paul came to town and began preaching against pagan idols, which threatened Demetrius' work. It was big business, for Artemis' (Diana) temple was one of the Seven Wonders of the World and was larger than a football field. It had 127 pillars sixty feet high and gold for mortar between the stones' blocks. If Demetrius would convert to Christianity, he would have to stop his idolatrous work. Let me just give some examples of the way this works for us today using the following illustrations.

    a. A friend of mine quit a job at a weight loss clinic because they wanted her to promote products to people who didn't need them and couldn't afford them.

    b. A friend of mine complained about the employer's treatment of his seriously injured dog and his treatment of another employee, and she was fired.

    c. People have been hurt or lost employment because they said something about irregular practices at the office: people taking equipment or abusing phone and machine privileges.

    d. I have known police officers who were expected to "look the other way" so as not to "blow the whistle" on fellow officers and violate the unspoken bond of fraternal, "good old boy" network.

    e. One friend was asked by management to lie to clients. The alternative was to suffer at work.

f. What if you are the only ball player on the team who doesn't participate in the superstition of turning your cap around ("rally caps") in the dugout in order to bring the team good luck? Will your teammates take it congenially?
g. Kids at school face serious peer pressure to join in some inappropriate activities.

There will be times when a Christian will be called to choose between morality and money or friends.

M-5. God Doesn't Always Play Fair

Purpose Statement: *God's rules and our rules for justice, peace, and human relationships aren't always the same.*

We say God's ways are different from our ways and we don't always understand them. In many situations we do understand God's way; we just don't like it. Jesus teaches some ideas that seem unpalatable to us. One such example is the Matthew 20:1-16 story we often label, "The eleventh hour workers." The employer pays all the employees the same wage, those who worked all day and those who only worked one hour. That rankles our sense of fairness. Then Jesus makes that ridiculous statement about the first being last and the last, first. And we ask why we aren't in charge of the universe.

a. We see desires and God sees needs. We worry about others getting as much or more than we do. God wants all persons to have their needs met. We see welfare as foolish freebees for the lazy. God sees welfare as caring for people.
b. We see reward and God sees love. We may not appreciate the thief on the cross getting some eleventh hour salvation. We worked hard or were faithful all our lives for our salvation. It isn't fair. The prodigal son is celebrated after his debauchery. We, the elder brother, are not happy about it. We see getting what we deserve as just. God says we love others so much that we are happy for their good fortune.

174

c. We see punishment and God sees forgiveness. We know people should be punished for their sins, while God talks about forgiveness. Where is the justice? Matthew 5:38-48 strongly suggests capital punishment is wrong, as do all industrialized and educated countries except the United States. God says we must never practice vengeance. Hate only destroys us.

We say God's unfair ways won't work. Yet they have worked when we tried them.

M-6. Why Didn't Jesus Write A Bible?

Purpose Statement: *The real subject is our response to the written word and the living word.*

Most founders of religions wrote something, some even extensive "sacred" writings. Given a chance to make requests, many Christians would ask for some written document unaltered and direct from Jesus' hand. Of all people who have ever lived, he is the one we would want to have written a book. But he didn't write anything to our knowledge.

a. He may have anticipated his followers would do it, though not necessarily. We can speculate that some of them may have been writing down something at the time or shortly after. Though the Gospels were written between thirty and seventy years after Jesus' death, they may have been enlarged from early jottings of some of his followers.

b. The written word is often misunderstood and abused. Mark 8:14-21 is one example among many in the Gospels where the disciples of Jesus had serious difficulty understanding him. And they were visiting with him face-to-face with opportunities for clarifying questions. Think how often the Bible is made to say two entirely different things, or to support two contradictory issues. The words are there in front of us and we misunderstand, intentionally ignore, distort, or misinterpret the meaning.

175

c. Christianity is a way of life, not words. It is the living word that counts, when the Bible lives through our actions and lives. Jesus clearly emphasized that Christianity is not rules and laws, but rather a lifestyle. It is a living spirit within us. A written document may lead to legalism just as the Old Testament did for the Pharisees, and just as we sometimes allow the Bible to do to us today.

d. What more is needed than "The Great Commandment," the cross, and the resurrection? Jesus' summary of the law (Mark 12:28-34) is not spelled out in detail and yet, if we are serious and intentional about it, there is not much doubt what it requires of us. The cross and resurrection proclaim loudly the intended message. Without the Bible, the oral tradition would live on as it has at various times in the past. The rest of the written teaching of Jesus is icing on the cake, albeit really, really great icing.

M-7. You Have The Right To Remain Silent

Purpose Statement: *What we should do about gossip, media misinformation, or innuendos.*

Jesus had strong words about our careless words. What we say is held against us (Matthew 12:36-37). I think the parable of the enemy sowing weeds among wheat (Matthew 13:24-30) has to do with gossip and harmful words. The book of James (3:1-12) also has harsh things to say concerning our conversations. The tongue can start a fire and is hard to control.

a. Don't spread gossip. You have the right (better, obligation) to remain silent. We must bite our tongue for it is difficult to refrain from sharing something we heard that we shouldn't hear or share. We like to have interesting things to tell others. We like to show others we are "in the know." We feel at times someone deserves to be embarrassed. We feel good in contrast by making others look bad.

b.   Don't believe everything you hear or see. Some information is false. Everyone is innocent until proven guilty. Facts get misconstrued and twisted by the repeated telling of a story. Parlor games have illustrated this. While driving down the street I once thought I saw a minister I knew going into an x-rated theatre. It only looked like him and I had to tell myself I was probably wrong. Remember the story of the woman who accused one of the church members of being in a local tavern because she saw his wheelbarrow parked outside? The next night he intentionally left his wheelbarrow in front of her house all night.

c.   Don't let hearsay (or truth) affect relationships. If we truly love and care, we will never let something we have heard or thought we saw affect how we think or feel about, or how we act towards, another person. That is also the proper response even when the facts are true.

d.   Don't let the media get away with hurting persons. Censorship be darned (see H-3), the media has responsibilities, not only for free speech, but also for not hurting persons. Write, phone, or visit your local paper concerning stories that embarrass or hurt the reputations of others. Even when the person is finally exonerated, the innuendo or accusation, unfortunately, has tarnished the reputation and remains. How often we have heard a news story give a detailed account of an accident (a yellow plane leaving Little Rock at 12:08 this afternoon bound for Nashville carrying a couple and their son and daughter crashed and everyone was killed) and then say, "We are withholding the names until loved ones have been notified to protect them from anguish." I hear these stories and think hardly anyone wouldn't know from the description it was their family. We ask the question, "Is the press being sensitive at this point?"

177

M-8. Ladies, Let's Remember Our Places!

Purpose Statement: *Clergy must preach on the status of women in society and within the church.*

It is common knowledge that women have been oppressed throughout history as well as currently around the world. They have been denied education and other rights. They have been considered property and abused in many ways. Problems still exist today in our own country and even within the church. Salaries are not equal with men, promotions are not as available as they are for men, and in the church there is still room for growth.

    a. Give examples of inequalities. Mentioning the way women suffer in places such as Afghanistan is fine, but we must not ignore the problems that still exist in our own communities. There are churches that will not ordain women or allow them in the pulpit. And churches that do will still find some resistance from the congregations. We are slow to accept the rights and dignity of women.

    b. Women in the Old Testament. The Bible isn't perfect and there are shameful accounts of the mistreatment of women in the Old Testament. One example will suffice: Abraham passed his wife off as his sister to allow King Abimelech to sleep with her (Genesis 20:1-3). This is indicative of how women were valued. Knowing this makes the achievements of women in the Old Testament even more remarkable. While the second creation story is sexist (Genesis 2:4b-24), the first is not (Genesis 1:1-2:4a, note verses 26-27). Deborah (Judges 4 and 5) was a judge, prophetess, and great military commander in Israel. Huldah (2 Kings 22:8-21) was a prophetess and the first person to pronounce a part of our Bible to be Bible. Judith (of the Apocrypha book by that name) was a great leader for Israel.

    c. Women in the New Testament. Except for some careless remarks by Paul, the New Testament does better by women. Galatians 3:28 tells us there is neither male nor female. Paul lists many early church leaders who were women:

Phoebe, Priscilla, Claudia, etc. Women were prophetesses, deacons, and teachers. Jesus elevated the status of women by the way he visited openly and freely with the woman at the well (John 4). Jesus had women as followers who traveled with him and his disciples, and even apparently handled the finances (Luke 8:1-3). The fact that Luke did not use the term "disciple" for them was his bias. Jesus' reference to God as Father is a cultural identification to the people of his day.

d. Give suggestions how the church can help improve the status of women today.

M-9. Did Jesus Drink?

Purpose Statement: *It is possible Jesus did not use alcoholic beverages and the Bible does not support social drinking. If this were true, it would suggest that Christians should abstain.*

Given the nature of Jesus, from any way you look at it, it seems highly improbable that Jesus would have used any intoxicating drinks. Alcohol is so totally destructive in our society and Jesus is so concerned with the welfare of people, that it seems totally out of character and highly unlikely he would use anything that has that kind of devastating consequences when it is not one of life's necessities. On the other hand, the Bible seems to have too many references that indicate there is nothing wrong with the use of alcohol. How do we resolve this difficulty? There could be three points to develop this message:

a. The use of alcohol is so destructive to society. There is so much written material describing the evils of drinking alcohol. You can quote statistics revealing its terrible effects on family life and personal relationships, its involvement in a high percentage of automobile accidents, its connection with so much crime, and so forth. It serves no good purpose and isn't one of life's necessities. Ridding society

179

of alcohol could only bring significant benefits. (See sermon E-10 for evidence that Prohibition worked!)
b. Jesus would never use it or condone it. Develop the obvious fact the Jesus stood for everything that benefits society and nurtures people, and against everything that is harmful. (Matthew 11:18-19 is accusatory, not proven. Jesus would not have been a "glutton" either.)
c. What does the Bible tell us? Of the many passages that speak of "wine" as negative, Proverbs 20:1; 23:20-21, 29-35; Habakkuk 2:15 16; Psalm 75:8; Hosea 7:5; Revelation 14:10; Isaiah 5:22; and 28:7-8 are a few. The most telling scriptures are Romans 14:13-21, 1 Corinthians 8:9-13, and Ephesians 5:18.

Bible Wines: or Laws of Fermentation and Wines of The Ancients, by William Patton (a book that seems to be of sound scholarship, but unfortunately may be out of print), explains that there is only one word for "wine" in scripture. It refers to both intoxicating drink and simple grape juice! Only by examining the context of the biblical passage can one determine which drink is implied.

(Note: My scholarly friend, Jerry McInnis, brought to my attention that the grape harvest was in the fall. The Passover was in the spring. It would have been difficult to have unfermented grape juice at the Last Supper.)

M-10. So, What?

Purpose Statement: *What is the reason for the cross and what does the cross do for us?*

The cross rivals the resurrection as the most important event in the life of Jesus. We talk so much about Jesus' death on the cross; it might behoove us to ask how much the average church member knows about it. Each of us can give some theory for what the cross does for us, but how deep have we probed into the issue?
a. Why the cross? I have sorted out four possible alternatives available to Jesus after his enemies decided to kill him.

First, he could have used his powers to defeat them and avoid dying on the cross. Jesus states clearly this was not his method (John 18:36). Secondly, he could have promised not to go on preaching and doing the things that irritated the authorities. Of course, that would be impossible; he could not give up his mission. Thirdly, he could have run away and hidden to evade arrest and death. Again, this would be impossible; we would lose all respect for him. Finally, he could face the cross and say, "I will remain firm in my ministry even if it means I will die for revealing God's love to you. It will be one more way, the ultimate way, to show you how far God's love will go for you."

b.   Some theories of the cross. There are various theories concerning just what the cross accomplishes. They blend together and deserve careful scrutiny. The worst possible suggestion is that Christ had to ransom us from the devil, which he then apparently cheated out of his prey. Another is that God was displeased with our sins and Jesus took the punishment we deserved to free us and now God likes us again. This one has subtle little variations, none of which satisfy some Christians regarding the loving nature of God. These ideas are sprinkled here and there in the New Testament (Romans 3:25-26, Hebrews 9:28, and elsewhere). I like the simple idea expressed by an early church father, Abelard (1079-1142), who said he rejected other theories such as the ransom to the Devil, etc., and put forth the thought that it was simply an act of love for us. Jesus was saying, "This is how far I will go to remain faithful to my teaching and reveal God's love for you." It is called the "moral influence" theory. As powerful as I deem this to be, it does not go far enough to satisfy some Christians.

c.   The cross isn't automatic. Whatever recipe appeals to you, the cross does nothing for us until we respond in some way. If it buys forgiveness or reveals love, etc., I am not saved, am not forgiven, or am not converted, until I accept what happened on the cross and allow it to claim me. I must be moved, respond, accept, be influenced, trust, believe, or whatever it takes to make me change, be renewed, or reborn.

d. What will the cross do for you? Not every Christian has actually thought about what the cross does for her or him and what kind of response is necessary to make it happen. It is not a matter of some theological theory or what the church says about the meaning of the cross. It is simply and finally a personal response and decision each person must make. We must ask them, "What has the cross done for you?"

N.

N-1. God Thought You'd Never Ask

Purpose Statement: *Most Christians are not very serious about look-ing for God or receiving help unless they are in dire circumstances.*

Matthew 7:7-11 offers a great promise. Jesus says to ask, seek, or knock and God will respond. He goes on to say that we as parents know how to meet our children's needs with love, and God's love and gifts are far greater. It finally dawned on me that our situation with God is exactly like the game show, *Jeopardy*. This show has turned it all around by giving the answers and the contestants must respond with the correct question. (In reality, they are fooling no one. Basically, the contestants are given questions and respond with answers. Because *Jeopardy* switched the names around means nothing.) Nevertheless, God provides the answers and we must come up with the correct questions! Most of us fail to take God up on the promise. We must:

    a.   Be concerned enough to ask. In many cases, people only get involved in social action over an issue that touches them personally. If they are not directly affected, people will generally not be very interested in the cause. It may take something out of the ordinary to catch our attention and motivate us to become involved. When frustration sets in, the problem gets too big, or we feel offended, we look for help.

    b.   Know what to ask. What would most people pray for or desire? Perhaps money, popularity, success, our team to win, something bad for our enemies, more free time, and more along these lines. How high on our list would be such things as knowing the right side on a controversial issue, really providing food for the hungry, strength and patience for each day's Christian witness, a greater sense of wonder about our universe, or finding a new way to serve?

c. Recognize the answers. If we offered an appropriate prayer and it was answered, would we even know it? Do we dismiss answers as coincidence or luck? Sometimes we are searching for an answer or solution, when we *are* that answer "walking around ready to happen," and we don't know it.

d. Believe the answers. The answer might easily be different than what we expected or wanted, and thus relegated to a non-answer status. Our values are so often different from God's values that we would not believe the right answer. *Hagar the Horrible* (a comic strip about a bungling Viking) was asked by his peace-loving son, "How can we have peace in the world?" Hagar answers, "It isn't easy, son; we have to constantly fight for it."

Will you be asking God any new questions this week?

N-2. Is The Real You The Right You?

Purpose Statement: *Do we know who we really are, and more importantly, what we can become?*

Remember the situation concerning the animal cage at the zoo with the sign on it that read, "The most dangerous animal in the world"? In the cage was a mirror. Some introspection or self-examination could reveal some real surprises about ourselves. The better the Christian knows himself or herself and his or her potential, the healthier their spiritual life will be. James 1:22-25 discusses how hard it is to know ourselves unless we listen to God and then practice being what God wants us to be. Do you know your many selves?

a. As you see yourself. There is a side of us that only God and we know. Many people do not like who they think they are. This often comes from perceptions of how we think the world perceives us, and we want to come across much better.

b. As others see you. You never know for sure exactly how others view you; you can only suspect. We ask our best friends subtle questions hoping for some glimmer. It is important to us as social animals to be accepted by some valued group and feel that we belong and are worthy.

c. As you want others to see you. We wear masks and try to fool other people in order to give a better impression of who we are. This image we want to portray to others changes radically depending on who those others are. Being a hypocrite means trying to convince others you are something that you are not. However, when the motive is good, such as trying to make a Christian witness, or seeking to help another when you know it is the right thing to do, even when you don't want to, that is not hypocrisy.

d. As God sees you. God knows the real *us* better than we know ourselves — and God loves us anyway. The fact that we are human beings qualifies us for respect and love. God forgives and renews our spirits.

e. As God wants you to be. God has a plan for our potential as we were created "in God's image" (Genesis 1:26-27, 31). The trick is to find that image God knows you can be! We aren't very successful at this endeavor. (Teens get involved in drugs and other undesirable behavior supposedly seeking "to find themselves." That has become just a handy catchphrase to excuse unwarranted activities.) God can start with the unlikely and make us very lovable. Moses was disabled. Ruth was a foreigner. Paul was "afflicted" with a serious health problem. David was small and ruddy — and a wicked sinner. Mary was very poor. Peter was impetuous and clumsy. Matthew was a traitor. John the Baptist was eccentric.

N-3. The Ninth Beatitude: Blessed Are Those Who Get Angry!

Purpose Statement: *It is not always wrong to get angry.*

The Beatitudes are so gentle and peaceful that it not only seems, but also is incongruous to propose one that lifts anger to the status of a virtue. We find ourselves confused over the propriety of anger. We have been told that it is definitely wrong. While I wouldn't give a blanket endorsement to the idea that there is a time for every activity as Ecclesiastes 3 suggests, I would say that there is a proper time to get angry. There is no better example than that given in John 2:13-17 where, shortly after Jesus hits town, he is in the Temple and angry over the moneychangers and animal sellers. I believe Jesus' actions give us permission to become angry. The only question is: What are the limits — the when and how? I would suggest these requirements for appropriate anger:

a. We get mad at activities and attitudes and not people. People are precious even when they do bad things. We hate actions that hurt others as well as the perpetrators, and still we must love the perpetrators. Our anger is motivated by our love for others, including the perpetrators. We are angry over the threat to their well-being.

b. If it is a just cause. We can dress anger up with more polite euphemisms such as "righteous indignation" or "determined moral concern," but the cause should be the same. Our goal is to right a wrong, to eliminate injustice, or correct an immoral outrage. It is not a matter of having God on our side, but trying to be sure we are on God's wavelength.

c. If no one gets hurt. Jesus did not beat the moneychangers and animal sellers with his whip. He used it to drive out the animals. Since our anger is directed to the well-being of others, we refrain from physical harm and personal insults. If, on occasion, physical restraint is called for and harm results, the harm must be less than the harm prevented. And most important, when the first opportunity arises, we immediately seek reconciliation.

d.   Love is never lost sight of. During the altercation, if possible, and certainly as soon as possible afterwards, we show the other persons our love for him. This means that we must constantly be aware of our own feelings and motives to be sure that love is always behind our actions.

N-4. David And Bathsheba: An Affair To Remember

Purpose Statement: *There is much to learn from this story of loyalty, courage, sin, responsibility, punishment, and forgiveness.*

2 Samuel 11 records one of the most despicable events in history, and chapter 12 follows up with one of the bravest. David lusts after Bathsheba, has an affair with her, she becomes pregnant, and he has her husband killed so he can have her. Her husband Uriah, in the middle of the episode, displays supreme loyalty to his king, his country, and his fellow soldiers. In the next chapter (12) Nathan, the prophet, condemns David to his face and David is punished, though the punishment falls more on his family than him. There are different ways to select lessons from this event.

First, one could develop the ideas: 1) We are all sinners. 2) Some sins are worse than others. 3) God forgives even the worst kind of sins.

Or one could use the principles and what their lives teach: 1) David sinned in a very wicked way. 2) Uriah sacrificed his own pleasures in order to remain loyal. 3) Nathan did an exemplary thing in scolding and shaming his king to his face.

Or one could focus on David in this way:

a.   The Bible never glosses over the sins of its heroes. I really appreciate this fact concerning our scriptures. One could go through the Bible and learn of the faults of many of its heroes. That is rare in the sacred literature of other religions, and other literature as well. Wickedness of this magnitude is usually ignored or partially sanitized. Two other examples, among many in our Bible, of the shameless exposure of the sins of great religious leaders would include

Abraham's offering his wife to Abimelech because he was afraid (Genesis 20, and the same sin is repeated by Isaac in Genesis 26), and Paul's shaming of Peter because of his racism (Galatians 2:11-14).

b. We cannot gloss over our sins because of the sins of the heroes. It is easy to excuse our sins in the light of the fact that the great Bible heroes were guilty of worse ones. But it won't work.

c. God's forgiveness did not gloss over the hero's punishment. David was punished in several ways.

N-5. Famous Flights: The Art Of Running Away

Purpose Statement: *Running away from a problem is not always bad.*

Matthew 2:13-15 is only one of some very famous flights in our Bible. The parents of Jesus were warned to go to Egypt because Herod was planning to kill infants to ward off threats of a future king. So a little girl came home from Sunday school with a drawing she had made of a Bible story. Her father, seeing an airplane in the picture, asked her what Bible story had an airplane in it. She said it was the "flight to Egypt." She pointed out Mary, Joseph, and baby Jesus. Her father asked, "Who is this flying the plane?" "That is Pontius Pilot," she replied. Since our Bible has so many instances of running away, and we talk about it so much, it seems appropriate for consideration.

a. Unfortunately, running away is seen as bad. And too often it is an ugly burden placed on children. They are shamed for running away from a fight. To run away is being a coward or a quitter, we are told.

b. At times, however, running away is best. Looking at any number of biblical flights, we can see the prudence in avoiding danger or impossible situations. Moses fled, Abraham left his original country, Jacob and family ran from a famine to Egypt, Jeremiah fled to Egypt, Jesus' family fled to

Egypt (a popular refuge, apparently), David ran away from Saul, and the disciples in the garden ran. (Mark, they say, was so frightened he ran away naked.) These incidents were all wise choices. "One who fights and runs away lives to fight another day."

c. The secret is to know when. A famous country western song is right on the mark, "You have to know when to hold 'em, and when to fold 'em." Some "running away" examples are not good; Jonah comes to mind. There is a time when we stay and deal with the situation, when we know we have the resources and have an opportunity to win a battle. Rosa Parks and Martin Luther King, Jr., picked the right time. "Turning the other cheek" and "going the second mile" are not running away instructions. Pick your battlegrounds carefully. For example: traffic arguments are not prudent. Leave; the other driver may shoot you!

N-6. If Crows Don't Worry, Scarecrows Won't Work

Purpose Statement: *Apparently stress or worry is one of our greatest burdens and needs consideration from the pulpit.*

One interesting "bulletin blooper" read: "Don't let worry kill you — let the church help." Stress, exacerbated during holiday seasons, we're told, robs life of a great deal of enjoyment, satisfaction, and peace. At times, it is even fatal. There are people who cannot even enjoy the good times because they worry about what could come along and spoil it. Persons anticipating a visit from their children who live some distance will lose much of the pleasure because of worry over the possibilities of an accident on the highway. Paul (2 Corinthians 4:8), a man who experienced far more rough times than most of us do, said that he had his doubts and troubles, but never let it get him down. Jesus makes a clear statement in Luke 12:22-31 concerning stress and worry. Jesus first makes two comments just a few verses earlier (vv. 4, 6-7) about not being afraid even of those who can kill the body and about

God's caring about the sparrows, thus consequently more about us. Jesus goes on to say we should not worry. Behold, the crows never worry (v. 24). Can we live longer because we worry (v. 25)? We will probably not live as long if we worry.

    a. We are more in control than we think. We worry because we do not know what fate will bring. In actuality, we control the effects of worry. If crows aren't afraid of scarecrows, they won't be effective in keeping the crows away. If we deal maturely and reasonably with worries, worry can be conquered. It is up to us. Much of what troubles us is the possibilities that never happen. The only way they will hurt us is when we worry about them. It is a matter of perspective.

    b. Some tips for stress control. Such suggestions pop up everywhere. We are only borrowing them and adding our faith to the list. Ways to control worry and stress include:

1. Keep busy (good busy, not bad busy).
2. Eat properly.
3. Cultivate hobbies.
4. Get appropriate exercise.
5. See problems as opportunities.
6. Get good rest.
7. Practice relaxation exercises.

Then:

Maintain a healthy prayer life, worship seriously, and begin to think of others more than of self. Start early. Don't wait until after the fire to install fire alarms.

The Beak of the Finch, by Jonathan Weiner, has some very cute illustrations from the Galapagos. Sometimes the birds would fly up onto the head and shoulders of the author and friends for protection when they spotted a hawk. What frightens you? What do you worry about?

190

N-7. Things To Do During A Dull Sermon

Purpose Statement: *What is the proper way to respond to sermons?*

Our sermons are never dull, are they? I remember seeing a book with the title "101 Things To Do During A Dull Sermon" or something to that effect. The suggestions, if I remember correctly, included ideas such as rolling marbles across the floor, sending a note of requests up to the organist, and slapping someone really to test the "turn the other cheek" theory. We have all been guilty (if it is a sin) of being bored during a sermon or two. The following are considerations for boring as well as exciting sermons, and everything in between.

a. How would you do it? Ask yourself the following questions. If I were preaching the same subject or ideas, how would I organize my thoughts? What illustrations could I use? How could I say it in a more interesting way?

b. Try to challenge the ideas. I like to hear or read what the other side is saying — those whose beliefs are diametrically opposed to my position. I enjoy arguing mentally, trying to build a case against what I am hearing or reading. Are there any holes in my logic? Where are the holes in the other argument?

c. Let the ideas challenge you. Do we need to change? Certainly, there must be room for us to improve or grow. What are those ways? You may not like the ideas. But we should all try to examine our life and beliefs regularly by the challenges from, among other things, sermons. Are we in denial? Is something being said that is necessary for us to hear and we are avoiding the issue?

d. Remember the sermon is not everything. Church is not the sermon, nor the preacher. Worship is hymns, personal prayers, scripture, and fellowship with other Christians as your church family. The sermon is a small part, and the preacher will move someday.

N-8. Tell Me How You Know There Is A God

Purpose Statement: *Make an interesting list of the evidence for God's existence.*

Some, maybe most, Christians once in a while have their doubts about the existence of God. The reason is that God is invisible and inscrutable. We know a great deal about God from Jesus, but mostly only as it relates to our moral life. Beginnings, futures, and infinity in space and time — all a part of God — are just too enigmatic. (The minister might begin this message with definitions for deism, atheism, agnosticism, anthropomorphic, and incarnation.) Honest persons will admit to their doubts and it is good to deliberate on the following exercise. Here is a partial list of evidence for God.

a. Jesus revealed God (John 14:1-20). We must accept this on faith. Faith is not evidence; it is conviction without evidence. This scripture is quite a full description of Jesus' relationship with and revelation of God.

b. Creation. Nothing happens without a cause. Even children will ask, "Well, then who created God?" That is an enigma because our minds cannot grasp infinity or forever. A God who always was is more reasonable than the universe coming from nothing.

c. Design. The eye, the heart, the brain, intricate physical laws, the unbelievable balance of life, and what is needed for life speak of a design not possible just by chance.

d. Ladder of goodness (and life). There are all degrees of goodness and a hierarchy of living things. The epitome is perfection in goodness and fullness of life. Put these two together and you do not have an abstract, but a living, reality.

e. Moral order. Kant spoke of the law of sin and punishment built into the universe.

f. Justice. If there is no God, this is the cruelest of all possible possibilities. Pain and suffering and sin would be in control with no chance for justice in an afterlife.

g. Anselm's argument. He posed a "something of which nothing greater can be conceived" which has to be God. This is too deep for me, so, moving on ...

h. Instinct. A need for God and a belief for such are inherent in us. Would this be if there were no God?

i. Law of love. Perhaps related to Kant's moral order, the presence of love and even sacrificial love is proof of the spiritual law existing in the universe. And God is love.

j. Personal experience. Sensing the presence of God with us and in us, and the experience of prayer may be the only evidence we need.

Interestingly enough, the Bible never feels the need to "prove" God or argue for the existence of God. It is entirely assumed.

N-9. Cupid's Arrow

Purpose Statement: *How do we know our love is the real thing?*

In our New Testament, there are at least five words used for some form of love. *Eros* means sexual love, *storge* signifies family affection, *philanthropia* denotes humanitarianism, *philia* stands for friendship, and *agape* is the love God has for us. We probably work with only two types of love generally: sensual or romantic love, and a "Platonic" or friendship kind of love. One basic question concerning love can be troublesome: How do we know that our love is authentic? The same question applies for any kind of love, and for others' love for us as well as our love for them. To help answer that question we could not turn to any better passage in our scriptures than the "love chapter," 1 Corinthians 13. There are several tests or ways of knowing, but I would focus on four that appear in the fourth and fifth verses. One could include that love is not proud, conceited, kind, irritable, or jealous. I choose these:

a. Love is patient (v. 4). Love can wait and doesn't rush. This is a vital measure of the authenticity of the love one has for another. Someone who has two potential mates and doesn't yet know which one she or he "loves best" should

193

wait and let it work itself out. If one or both of the lovers pushes for a decision, then their love could be suspect. We also have an excellent test at our disposal for when we are pressured for sex and we feel our relationship is not that far along yet. We simply say, "No." If that doesn't suffice with our partner, we look askance at the relationship.

b. Love is not ill-mannered (v. 5). Love does not test others with the old "If you love me" ultimatum. Love is never rude, crude, or thoughtless.

c. Love is not selfish (v. 5). Love is never a matter of "what I want." It thinks of the other person and her or his needs and desires. Pushed to extreme, a person who is too passive and gives in to the other partner constantly is not in a healthy relationship and needs some counseling. When you care and share with the other, it should be reciprocal. If one person needs always to get his or her own way, this is a red flag for concern.

d. Love does not keep a record of wrongs (v. 5). Love is unconditional and always forgiving. This does not mean that you allow yourself to be taken advantage of. Love never brings up old problems or sins of the other; they must remain dead and buried.

These are excellent measures of a sincere and healthy love relationship. Jesus stated it profoundly and simply, "Love your neighbor as yourself."

N-10. Wrong ... For All The Right Reasons

Purpose Statement: *Occasionally, we are wrong, even when we believe we are right. This is due to ignorance.*

Each of us could recall times we were wrong when we thought we were right. We believed our reasons were accurate. It is also possible to be right when we think we are wrong.

a. Get all the facts. An unusual example is the classic betrayal in Luke 22:1-6, 47-53. Judas has been portrayed as a heinous traitor of the worst kind. There is no question he was wrong. Perhaps, however, under careful scrutiny we may have a more tolerant view of Judas and his motives. There is a theory that Judas' purpose was more altruistic or righteous than he is given credit for. Some say Judas was a zealot who believed Jesus to truly be the Messiah and betrayed him in order that he would be forced to use his powers in resistance and "bring in the kingdom." Far-fetched, you say? The evidence gives some credence to the theory. How could Judas work with Jesus so long and not be won over? The betrayal money was insignificant; he ended up throwing it away. Why did he kiss Jesus when he could have just pointed to him? Why did he hang himself? Was it because the plan, of Jesus being forced to use his powers to protect himself and reveal his Messiahship, failed? Was Judas not so bad after all, just wrong for all the right reasons? Immediately, one of the disciples uses a sword to attack the attackers, and Jesus has to stop him. Again, is this someone who was wrong for the right reasons?

b. There is some good in all persons. Judas could be an example of how there is some good in all persons. We tend to label a person who has done a sinful thing as a bad person. And Jesus reminds us continually, "Let the person who has not sinned throw the first stone."

c. This makes us more cautious and tolerant. The lesson is: Be careful not to be too quick to judge and act. It should also make us a little more humble, ourselves. Think of the innocent persons we have executed by capital punishment.

0.

O-1. What Does God Promise?

Purpose Statement: *What exactly can we count on from God?*

We hear about the promises of God. The opening line of the famous hymn is "Standing on the promises of Christ my King," and the closing line is "I'm standing on the promises of God." It speaks of eternity, strength in trials, and rest. Have you ever sat down to draw up a list of what God promises? In the Old Testament we could find some promises such as: a land flowing with milk and honey, lots of descendents, being a chosen people, protection from enemies, and never having to worry about the world being destroyed by a flood again. As Christians, we should concentrate on the New Testament for our promises.

a. What God does not promise.

   1. Wealth. Being a Christian will not guarantee wealth and material possessions, although there are many Christians who still think so. But if wealth were a reward of faithfulness to God, we need only look at our world and see that the rich are the good people and the poor are the wicked people, all getting what they deserve.

   2. Health. This is the same as wealth. Obeying God does not bring good health, or else we could also look around and say the people who are well are the saints and the sick people are the wicked people. There must be an asterisk to this thought, however. Following a Christian lifestyle should entail taking care of your body as good stewards. Eating right, proper exercise, and good rest should bring some health rewards.

   3. Protection. None of the prophets and followers of Jesus were promised protection in any way, and they didn't get it. Jesus warned them of persecutions because they were faithful. And Jesus was not protected from suffering.

b. What does God promise? John 14:1-27 is one of many places in scripture where we can get some idea of the promises of God.
   1. Spiritual strength. Verse 27 tells us not to be afraid, for Jesus says he leaves us peace! We may not be spared troubles, but we will have God's presence and strength to see us through. So often in my ministry I have heard persons who suffer a great deal say, "I don't know how I would have gotten through this without God's help!"
   2. Guidance. Verses 16 and 17 speak of the spirit of God that Jesus leaves with us as a "counselor" that will be a guide for us. The teachings of Jesus provide the greatest possible answers to how we can live the moral life.
   3. Eternal life. At the heart of our faith, verses 2 and 3 assure us that God has promised us eternal life.

O-2. What Does God Require?

Purpose Statement: *God does expect certain responses and behavior from us. What are these?*

We know that God expects us to be a certain kind of person and to do certain things. Where is that list? How do we know? The Bible is filled with helpful ideas as well as outright commands. Some are easy to find: the Ten Commandments, the Beatitudes, and the Sermon on the Mount, while other ideas take a lifetime of Bible study and meditation. Some persons will simplify it all by saying, "Just accept Jesus." It needs some more elaboration. I will list two popular and profound statements concerning what God requires of us. These summarize the subject in a magnificent way.
   a. Micah 6:6-8. Micah even begins by saying this is what God requires.
      1. Do what is just. This means to build the kind of communities where people are all treated fairly and equally. This means social action. It means getting political. It

means spending time learning all about social issues and where the injustices are in our society.

2. Show constant love. The word "love" is overworked and actual love is under used. Loving other people leads to service. It means making sacrifices and seeing opportunities to care for others.

3. Live in fellowship with God. Nothing else is possible without this mandate. Finding God is finding the knowledge, courage, compassion, and strength to be a Christian in the world for others.

b. Matthew 22:34-40. Jesus says he is summarizing the law into these two statements.

1. Love God. Love God with all you have. God is our life, our all. Our life cannot be centered, wholesome, productive, and complete without a relationship with our Creator and the source of all love.

2. Love others. Jesus said these two ideas are one. If we love God, we will love others, and in the process of loving others, we love God. However, it is a stern and difficult proposal, to love our neighbor as our self. We commit to that ideal and then spend the rest of our lives praying and studying the teachings and life of Jesus to see how to do it.

O-3. Americanized Religion

Purpose Statement: *To show how our country's values, good and bad, have influenced our Christian church.*

There is so much radical patriotism running rampant in the United States, and it increases significantly during wartime or during real or suspected threats to our country. As Christians, we are to live in two worlds. We live here physically, but we are called to obey the will of God in God's Kingdom. The two do not always synchronize. The danger is that the Christian becomes too worldly, or takes on the values of the world even when they oppose God's values. Consequently, the values and principles of the United States begin to mold and influence Christians. When those are the values of radical patriotism, it distorts Christian values. Use Matthew 22:15-21 where Jesus says to give to the government (or nation) what belongs to the government, and to God what is God's.

a. The church becomes viewed as an arm of the nation. It is "God bless America over the rest of the world."

b. The nation's values influence the church. Values such as greed, competition, aggressiveness, toughness, rugged independence (opposite values from the church) make Christians vulnerable to the same problems as the nation as a whole. These problems make the United States a world leader in divorce, crime, citizens in jail, suicide, gun deaths, alcoholism, juvenile crime, broken homes, rape, domestic violence, drug use, the gap between the rich and the poor, and the only industrialized country to have capital punishment.

c. Christians begin to think like radical patriots. Super patriots (those who have carried good ideas to the extreme) create a divisive world where it is "we versus them." They have an artificial division where they can turn the guns on anyone at anytime when paranoia sets in. They don't care about people; just themselves. You won't see them at Hattiesburg or Selma or Montgomery unless it is unleashing the dogs on civil rights' activists. They don't allow criticism of our country. And criticism is often necessary for growth. Not only individuals, but also countries must admit faults and accept responsibility for wrongs.

d. Christians choose true patriotism. True patriotism (and Christianity) is love for all people as the children of God — one world. God is not for us; God is for everyone and for peace. It is an appreciation of all cultures. It is gratitude for the values of freedom and democracy because we respect people. It is an enjoyment of our country's natural beauty and a desire to share it with the world.

O-4. Religionized America

Purpose Statement: *To show how the Christian church has tried to control our nation's policies.*

It is natural to want to take advantage of privilege. If you can get something someone else can't, the feeling is "go get it!" In a competitive environment such as ours, it is believed good business or just good common sense to take advantage of being in control or in the majority. Christianity has that privileged status in our country. Use Matthew 22:15-21 as it deals with what belongs to God and what is due the state.

a.   First, many see our country as a Christian country. Unfortunately, much of the world has come to identify Western civilization as synonymous with Christianity. When we seek to share the Christian faith and ideals with the world, it sees the process (as we sometimes do) as converting the rest of the world to Western ways.

b.   Second, we claim the nation was founded by Christians, and from that deduce it was founded "for" Christians. There were deists among the founders and the nation was founded on separation of church and state and freedom for all religious peoples. No one religion was to have special privileges.

c.   Third, our biased perspective leads our Christian church to seek special treatment because we are in the majority. When we want scripture and prayer in the classroom or our legislatures, it is to be Christian scripture and prayer. Prayer at sports events is Christian prayer.

d.   Finally, the extension of this religionizing of America is the desire of the "religious right" to take over or have a monopoly. They would like to have their values imposed on all others because they are right and everyone else is wrong. There is no tolerance. Special privilege and control eliminates all semblance of religious freedom, or any kind of freedom.

O-5. Nobody Actually Takes The Bible Literally

Purpose Statement: *Biblical interpretation is a major thorn in the Christian church. How one interprets scripture causes dissention and division in the church.*

Because of the above statement, it is vital that Christians become educated concerning this idea of "taking the Bible literally." In doing so, many Christians will be shocked by what they learn, or else they are incapable of thinking. Jesus castigated the Pharisees who were the religious leaders of his day (Matthew 23). Their forte was being meticulous in the interpretation of the law. They took their Bible literally. The fundamentalists (and I lump those "conservatives" who believe they take the Bible literally with the fundamentalists) are the Pharisees today, and they should read this chapter 23 carefully.

    a. Fundamentalists say take the Bible literally. There have always been serious arguments concerning Bible interpretation. More conservative Christians insist on taking scripture literally for very good reason. They have a legitimate fear that once you fail to take some passage literally, the door is open to questioning all passages, and our faith might collapse. We are all sophisticated enough to understand when something in someone's conversation or in the media shouldn't be taken literally. Yet, this isn't so when it pertains to scripture. Sophistication and reason go out the window. Somehow we cannot see myth, analogy, fictitious illustrations, exaggeration, and other devices the Bible authors used as they spoke figuratively.

    b. However, fundamentalists don't and liberals do. Sometimes, anyway. There are so many examples in scripture where the fundamentalist must "interpret," manipulate, ignore, or add details that do not exist. In these cases the liberal simply takes it literally. The deaths of Saul and Judas are good examples. 1 Samuel 31 and 2 Samuel 1 give two stories concerning Saul's death. The liberal simply takes them literally and says they are two different traditions and there are some mistakes. The "literalist" finds a loophole: for example, someone is lying — although the Bible does not say that. The same is true of Judas' death (Matthew 27:3-5 and Acts 1:18). The literalists cannot take the accounts literally, but must add some information or twist the meaning. Fundamentalists do not take the creatures in Revelation literally, nor the "numbers," days, etc., in Daniel. They do not interpret Isaiah 7:10-25 as the liberals do, as actual history happening in about 720 B.C. Instead they see it as figurative language about the future. Fundamentalists will not take passages such as Acts 28:1-6 (we can handle poisonous snakes and not be hurt) and Mark 16:18 (we can drink poison and not be harmed) literally. Or at least they are not willing to prove it.

c. Actually we all do and we all don't. We all take some passages literally and some figuratively. The unfortunate thing is that we can't agree on which. For example, if conservatives could take the passage from Acts 4:12 (that no one can be saved apart from belief in Jesus) a little more loosely, and less legalistically, they would be more tolerant and understanding.

O-6. Nobody Actually Takes The Bible Seriously

Purpose Statement: *Everyone reveres the Bible as the Word of God and more important than any other book, and yet few act as if they believe that.*

a. We don't read it. Many mainline Christians and most peripheral church members never read scripture. The only Bible they get is what the preacher reads on Sunday if they are in church. And, unfortunately, those who read the Bible faithfully and regularly, read only certain passages, or read with a jaundiced eye. There are some who do a very good job of studying scripture, and are able to do so with an open and critical mind. They are the ones who grow intellectually and spiritually. They are in the minority.

b. We don't obey it. There are so many commandments, laws, principles, and suggestions for our behavior which we simply ignore. It would seem if we took the teachings of scripture seriously, we would make concerted efforts to follow those dictums. Matthew 6:19 tells us not to store up possessions here on earth. Proverbs 25:21 (and other places in the New Testament as well) tells us to feed our enemy. Luke 12:33 tells us to sell everything and give the money to the poor. 1 Corinthians 14:5 has Paul saying he would like all of us to speak in tongues, and in verses 34-35, women should not speak in church. However, the Bible doesn't always obey itself. Adulterers are to be put to death, yet Rahab (Joshua 2) and David and Bathsheba (2 Samuel 11) are spared. Each of us probably has special loopholes so as to avoid obeying unpalatable biblical demands. Are they honest reasons or convenient evasions?

c. We don't believe it. Apparently. Since we don't read it honestly and there are passages we won't obey, one could suspect we don't believe it is the Word of God. Revering the Bible while ignoring its teaching does not excuse us from responsibility. It is like waving the flag as a patriot while not treating our neighbors — all our neighbors — with dignity, respect, and justice. Some sermon ideas are applicable to only part of our listeners, but getting serious with our Bible study and practicing its dictates are suggestions relevant for all of us.

O-7. How Good Was Jesus With A Sword?

Purpose Statement: *Did Jesus mean what he said about dividing a family, one member against another?*

A pastor could do an extensive series of sermons on puzzling or enigmatic statements that Jesus made. Some of his comments seem contradictory to God's love or to common sense. How do you explain them? One such passage is Matthew 10:34-39 where Jesus tells us he did not come to bring peace to the world, but that he came to bring a sword. He intends to set members of families against each other. These are very strong words in light of our inordinate concern today with "family values."

    a. Jesus is for family unity. The comments in this passage are certainly out of character for Jesus. Jesus is always speaking about God's love and our need to love one another. He gives examples such as the son who returned home after his rebellion and was forgiven and accepted joyfully by his father. The Good Samaritan story reveals an unusual care and compassion. Jesus says we must love our neighbor just as we love ourselves. Love, unity, peace, and harmony for family, friends, and even strangers permeate all of the teachings of Jesus. We can test all of his teachings for consistency; if they do not seem consistent, they are not authentically his or else we do not yet understand them. I'm sure these words are his, and when we understand them, they are in keeping with his total message.

    b. Jesus didn't actually bring a sword. It is others who provide the sword. Jesus simply said there are occasions when we cannot avoid the sword that others provide. The idea behind this passage is that each person must obey God and remain faithful to God's will as she or he understands it no matter what others think. We must stand for justice and morality even if it disrupts the family or breaks up friendships. Some illustrations will help:

       1. In a business the family owns and operates, there are some very unethical practices. You as a family member take a stand opposing the practice, saying, "We cannot cheat people!" The rest of the family doesn't understand, and excludes you as a traitor to family affairs. You have a choice: remain by your Christian convictions and break with the family (they do the fracturing), or compromise and be dishonest.

2. You forgive someone the family has a feud with, and show that person love. The family becomes angry and shuns you.
3. You take a strong position on a social issue that is opposed to that which your family takes. They don't understand your support and work for something that angers them. The family is split.
c. Jesus still brings peace. Given a choice of obeying God's will or pleasing your family or friends, you always choose God's will. It is not your intention (nor God's, nor Jesus') to divide the family; it is their choice. For your part, you must remain loving and reconciling even through your differences.

O-8. Try It — Perhaps God Hasn't Heard That Excuse Yet

Purpose Statement: *We must honestly confront our own excuses for avoiding God, not attending church, turning down a task in the church, not witnessing, or putting off discipline and commitment. Are they legitimate or phony?*

Excuses such as "I'm tired," "I'm retired," "I'm sick," "I'm too old," "I'm busy," "I didn't know," "I'm not capable," and so forth, usually won't do. Moses had an extensive and impressive list of excuses, and God met each one, one after the other, with a rebuttal (Exodus 3 and 4). Can you do better than Moses? Several would-be followers of Jesus had excuses (Luke 9:57-62) and Jesus wasn't impressed. This message is concerned with excuses for our sins.
a. Everybody else is doing it. We can't sneak by with the crowd. It may seem to make it easier to do wrong when it is common practice, but it is still just as wrong and we are just as guilty. Don't take any solace in fellowship in crime. We may be the one voice needed to witness for the right. Remember the salt of the earth and light of the world?

b.   If I don't, someone else will. Add a little more greed to the
     crime. It is analogous to the people wanting to justify the
     introduction of gambling in their state with the reasoning:
     our state residents are taking our state's money across the
     border to the next state to gamble. If I don't grab that
     twenty-dollar bill off the counter, someone else will.

c.   It's not as bad as other sins. That is why we appreciate
     convictions and executions; it makes our sins seem cleaner.
     That may be true, but it is still sin. Stealing ten dollars is
     not as bad as rape, but it still makes us a thief.

d.   I already did it once; another time won't hurt. This is the
     secret to breaking our diet. This kind of thinking makes it
     hard to quit smoking. Sinning once does make it easier to
     sin twice, but sinning twice will make it even easier a third
     time. We are doing dishonorable things on our way to be-
     coming a basically dishonorable person who cannot be
     trusted.

e.   No one will know. We will know and God will know.
     Wrong is wrong even when no one knows. And eventually
     when our sins over time have helped make us a dishonest
     person, others will find out.

O-9. Aaron's Instant Bull

Purpose Statement: *No one relishes being blamed for or taking
responsibility for sin.*

One of the great stories of the Old Testament is found in Exodus 32:1-24 where Moses is on the mountain getting the Ten Commandments from God. His brother, Aaron, is down below being
bullied by the crowd into giving them a new god to worship. "We
don't know if Moses is ever coming back." Aaron creates a golden
bull to appease their idolatry. When Moses finds out (and drops
and breaks the commandments) and gets angry with Aaron, Aaron
responds with another one-liner that ranks up there with the best
humorous comments in scripture. He answers, "I put this gold in

the fire and out comes this bull." Why, it almost makes God responsible, doesn't it? Here are some handy ways of avoiding responsibility for sin.

    a. Sin happens. Whenever we are blamed for wrongdoing, we look around for a quick fix, someone or something else to take the responsibility. And we find it convenient to divert blame, for sin is happening all around us. It is common. Everyone is doing it.

    b. Blame Eve. Try original sin. The claims of this doctrine are that you and I are born wicked. Because Eve sinned (some blame poor duped Adam), it was a sin for all time and for all people. Man (sic) fell and thus we are all born as sinners. I have never been comfortable with the concept of original sin. I believe it to be a faulty doctrine. No one sinned for me. I do all right by myself! I was not born a sinner or in a sinful state, nor was I born good or a saint. We were all born neutral with a clean slate and did not start to sin until we were old enough to know right from wrong. A baby's "selfishness" is not a sin. Eve did not start me on the road to ruin. The world is so filled with temptations that sin is easy. However, we bear sole responsibility for our wrongdoing.

    c. Just get over it. There was a great move a few decades ago, and it may still be with us, to say guilt was silly. "We should stop feeling guilty and get on with our lives." This philosophy, emanating from the psychology department, disturbed me. "An analyst will help you find out what you are feeling guilty over, and then you need to forget it. Stop letting it get in your way." How convenient. How foolish. Guilt is a necessary part of God's creation. 1) It makes us knowledgeable of sin, discerning right from wrong. 2) It causes us to be responsible for insults, wrongs, mistakes, and hurts to others. 3) It is necessary to recognize or there will be no real change, growth, or maturity. This careless philosophy (psychology) of uncovering guilt and forgetting it eliminates the repentance step necessary for becoming a new person. It dispenses with apologies and righting wrongs done to others. It ignores reconciliation. There is no instant bull in our lives; we created it.

O-10. Cain's And Einstein's Theory Of Relativity

Purpose Statement: *To show there are spiritual laws of the universe that are just as real as the physical laws and must be kept inviolate.*

Actually Einstein and I did not collaborate. In fact, we did not know each other well. As a matter of fact, we didn't know each other at all. In reality, when it comes down to it, I don't even understand the theory of relativity! I have no idea what Einstein was talking about. However, that does not invalidate my theory. And if you like, you may substitute your name in place of mine (Cain) above. You probably had the theory before I did anyway.

   a. There are spiritual laws of the universe that parallel the physical laws. There has been a move afoot for a long time that doesn't like laws. It leads to legalism, creates rigidity, eliminates flexibility, and misses the "spirit" of the discipline. Thus, it is fashionable to eschew "laws" and "rules" in favor of "positive attitudes." "Thou shalt nots" are not as motivating as an idea Jesus once shared, "Love God and your neighbor as you do yourself (Matthew 22:34-40)." And I agree. Nevertheless, there are indisputable physical laws in our universe, and I contend there are equal and parallel spiritual laws we must reckon with.

   b. Those spiritual laws are part of a "unified theory." Astrophysicists have been trying to unite all the physical laws of the universe into one neat package called the "unified theory." This unified theory seeks to pull into one theory the four or five all-embracing laws of the whole universe: nuclear, electro-magnetic, gravity, motion, and light and radiation. Where Einstein and his successors fail to pull it all together, I have succeeded in fashioning a "unified spiritual theory." The individual spiritual laws governing the universe include: honesty, faithfulness, sensitivity, kindness, and compassion. (You may have a different way of organizing virtues and values to encompass the broad spectrum.) These five laws are coalesced into a unified theory of "love." 1 John 4:7-13 states this theory nicely and says that God is love. Jesus summarized the spiritual laws into one (or two, he said they were the same one): Love God and neighbor (Matthew 22:37-40). It is a beautiful parallel of the physical laws of the universe.

c. The laws are polarized and balanced. There is a polarization in some physical laws such as the electro-magnetic where there are negatives and positives, opposites. We have the same properties in the spiritual laws such as the positive of love and its opposite, the negative, hate. There is a balance in physical laws. Gravity attracts the moon to the earth and keeps it from flying off into space. The laws of motion counteract the gravity and keep the moon from being pulled down and crashing into the earth. A delicate balance is maintained. In the spiritual realm we have similar balances. You love a child, but you also discipline a child. Ecclesiastes 3:1-8 reminds us of both the polarization and the balance.

d. The spiritual laws cannot be violated without automatic repercussions. Jump out of an airplane without your parachute and you will not successfully defeat the law of gravity. Spiritual laws are equally demanding. Violate the law of love by hating someone and you suffer. You may not always know it, but the consequences are real. By hating, a part of your soul is diminished. They say what you don't know won't hurt you — they're wrong. When we are selfish, dishonest, or unkind, we are punished by becoming a lesser human being. You reap what you sow (Galatians 6:7) is a law that cannot be beaten.

Subject Or Topic Index

214